The Constitution and the Delegation of Congressional Power

Sotirios A. Barber received his Ph.D. in political science in 1972 from the University of Chicago. He is now an associate professor at the University of South Florida (Tampa).

Sotirios A. Barber

The Constitution and the Delegation of Congressional Power

The University of Chicago Press
Chicago and London

The University of Chicago Press, Chicago 60637
The University of Chicago Press, Ltd., London
© 1975 by The University of Chicago
All rights reserved. Published 1975
Printed in the United States of America

Library of Congress Cataloging in Publication Data

Barber, Sotirios A.
    The Constitution and the delegation of congressional
power.

    Expanded and revised version of the author's thesis,
University of Chicago.
    Includes bibliographical references and index.
    1. Delegation of powers—United States. 2. United
States—Constitutional law. I. Title.
KF4565.B3   342'.73'044   74-16688
ISBN 0-226-03705-3

SOTIRIOS A. BARBER is associate
professor of political science at the
University of South Florida (Tampa).

to Sandy

Contents

Acknowledgments

Although the present book expands and revises the argument of my dissertation, submitted to the University of Chicago in 1971, my greatest debt is to those whose encouragement and criticism helped me formulate the original statement: Philip Kurland, Theodore Lowi, and Herbert Storing. I am grateful also to colleagues at the University of South Florida who read sections of the present manuscript: Jamil Jreisat, Janice Snook, Graham Solomons, and Sal Territo. Gail Albritton helped with final manuscript preparation. And I am grateful to my friend Jay Shuler for extensive help on matters of sytle. Fears of a lengthy acknowledgment prevent me from naming a number of other individuals who helped in various ways, from clerical assistance to discussions in class. Courtesies aside, I know this would have been a better book had I been more responsive to the criticisms of many of these individuals.

Introduction

From the early years of the Republic the courts have found implicit in the Constitution a rule restricting the degree to which Congress may delegate its powers to others. In this study we shall refer to this rule variously as the principle, doctrine, or rule of nondelegation. Against a background of continuing historical controversy over the status and proper scope of the rule, we shall seek to develop a general legal theory of what the rule ought to mean for the practice of Congress. We shall discuss a number of theoretical issues in this pursuit, including the constitutional status of what some have called a purely "judge-made" rule, its proper logical foundation, and its connections with norms like "separation of powers" and "due process of law." On the basis of a theory of its proper constitutional foundation and scope, we shall develop a set of guidelines for applying the rule to concrete acts of Congress. We shall employ these guidelines to evaluate several of the major delegation decisions of the United States Supreme Court. And we shall conclude with an attempt to determine whether the appropriations process, the legislative investigation, and other instruments of legislative oversight enable Congress to delegate beyond permissible limits and still serve the legal values supporting the delegation doctrine.

What, if any, are the constitutional limitations on the right of Congress to delegate its powers to others? This is the central and guiding question of this investigation. The current importance of this question is exhibited in such recent controversies as the constitutionality of the Vietnam War, the delegation of war powers to the president, the power of the president to impound appropriated funds, and the delegation to the president of control over wages and prices. The need for an answer to the delegation question is underscored by rising criticism from public figures, journalists, and scholars that Congress has "abdicated" much of its power and responsibility to the executive, the administrative agencies, the courts, and others. As chairman of the Senate Committee on Foreign Relations, J. William Fulbright cited the delegation of congressional authority as a principal factor in what he termed "presidential dictatorship" in the area of foreign policy.[1] The first publication of Ralph Nader's Congress Project criticized congressional performance generally as one of abdication and abuse, finding, for example, the delegation of congressional power to be a major factor in the presidential practice of impounding appropriations.[2] And a leading newsweekly has seen forfeiture of congressional power as a major factor in the "constitutional crisis" resulting from congressional decline in such areas as control of the budget, control of appropriations, and the determination of federal priorities.[3]

As commonplace as such criticism may have seemed in recent years, academic orthodoxy has had a different thrust for most of this century. Congress, so the orthodoxy goes, may have been equipped to handle the comparatively simple tasks of nineteenth-century government, but it is inadequate to the tasks of government today. Having come through a relatively passive era, modern government must do much more than provide mechanisms for defending the nation, expanding trade, settling civil disputes, and keeping order. In a greatly expanded number of areas, including transportation, communications, employment, wages and prices, labor relations, race relations, and the environment, modern government actively assumes responsibilities for promoting what it regards as the nation's physical, economic, social, and political health. Modern government is "positive government," and Congress is not equipped to govern the greatly expanded services of the positive state. For these reasons, the orthodoxy continues, Congress has been forced to delegate broad powers to those whose resources of expertise, time, information, and organization better equip them to serve modern needs. The courts, in turn, have modified the delegation doctrine in order to give broad delegations legitimacy in constitutional terms. As the need for broader delegations has increased over the years, the courts have upheld them under one rationalization or another. Although it has never openly rejected the delegation doctrine, the Supreme Court has employed it to invalidate congressional action only three times in its history.[4] These decisions came during a time of judicial hostility to the New Deal, and it is arguable whether they have continuing force today. The Supreme Court since the late thirties has consistently upheld broad delegations irrespective of their impact, a situation bringing some to the conclusion that the delegation doctrine is all but a dead letter of constitutional law.

Without rejecting all of the orthodox view, recent scholarship has insisted on amending it. It has been argued that, instead of always helping Congress achieve regulatory aims it may not otherwise achieve, broad delegations can defeat such purposes. The absence of reasonably clear statements of congressional policy has been seen as one of the conditions under which the independence of administrative agencies is threatened through the pressures of the groups they are supposed to regulate and the friends of these groups in Congress and the executive branch. As Henry J. Friendly explains it, "Lack of definite standards creates a void into which attempts to influence are bound to rush; legal vacuums are quite like physical ones in that respect."[5] While less sanguine than Friendly that clear policy choices by either Congress or the agencies are politically possible in certain high-conflict areas, Louis L. Jaffe notes the "evil consequences" of administrative confusion, unpredictability, and incoherence that sometimes result when Congress passes political hot potatoes to the agencies in the form of broad delegations. Jaffe notes a general decline in optimism over the potential of the administrative process, "buffeted" as the agencies are "by strong, opposing forces" which cause them to look for "compromise, expediency, and short-term solutions."[6] Theodore J. Lowi calls for an effective return to the prohibition of overly broad delegations. In the phenomena of congressional irresolution and resulting agency capture by clientele groups, Lowi sees the "atrophy of popular institutions," "the maintenance of old and creation of new structures of privilege," "strong resistance to change," and growing "political cynicism" among active observers of government.[7] Although the prominence of such criticism from the scholarly community is relatively recent, it is not entirely new. In reflecting on the failures of the National Industrial Recovery Act a generation ago, James M. Landis qualified his enthusiasm for the administration process with a warning against the hope that broad delegations to administrators could bail us out of the irresolution of legislators.[8]

As a result of such criticism, the wisdom of overly broad delegations has become a viable question once again. Pointing to the necessity of the administrative process is no longer sufficient to close the question. Nevertheless, it is going to be a difficult question for the nation to answer, perhaps profoundly difficult in some of its aspects. Congress, after all, delegates power for reasons which appear good to most of its members. These reasons can be politically compelling even when they fail to satisfy standards of official character and conduct that one would proclaim in public. Friendly has suggested that the unwillingness of Congress to provide clear statements of policy lies less in a lack of technical competence and time than in the desire of individuals to survive politically. He notes that while "pressure groups have long been with us.... the increased pluralism of our society and modern techniques of organization and communication have sharpened their impact on the legislator." In the face of such pressure, "the optimum is . . . to do nothing, since failure will be understood by those desiring the legislation whereas success will not be forgiven by those opposing." "If legislation there must be," continues Friendly, "the very necessity of a text arouses further opposition, hence the tendency to soften it in the sense of compromise or even of unintelligibility."[9] By delegating politically difficult decisions to others, Congress can disclaim responsibility if and when things go wrong. As one member of the Senate put it to the press, "We can delegate powers to the President, then sit back and carp or applaud, depending on whether what he does is popular or unpopular."[10]

If the politician's fear of electoral accountability motivates some of the delegations on which current criticism is focused, then "the delegation problem" subsumes more than questions concerning the competence of Congress, the executive, the courts, and other parts of government. The problem would also involve questions concerning the character of the electorate. At some point we might well find ourselves discussing the practicability of educating the electorate to value the buck passers in Congress less than those who do their duty even at the risk of electoral displeasure. Norms of "constitutional duty" would need to have a much stronger influence on public opinion than they do today. Can we realistically hope for development of such civic virtue in America? An effort to address this aspect of the delegation problem would immediately put us into an analysis of one of the central issues of the founding period: are we to rely for the maintenance of our institutions on a sense of duty among officeholders and their constituents, or on what Madison hoped would be a connection between personal ambition and the rights of office sufficient for ambition to check ambition and for making "the private interest of every individual ... a sentinel over the public rights"?[11] This issue is clearly present in some of today's efforts at reform. Ralph Nader, for example, has suggested that behind the decline of Congress is the people's "abdication" of the duties of citizenship. "By reclaiming the Congress," says Nader, "America revolutionizes itself. For in so doing there is a required build-up of citizenship, expertise, and stamina such as this country has never seen. It is the right and duty of every citizen to strive for such development. And it should not have to be the equivalent of reaching for the stars."[12] The philosophic and institutional issues in the background of such expectations certainly constitute the most interesting aspects of the delegation problem.

The delegation problem thus reveals itself to be a set of far-ranging and formidable issues. What, for example, were the expectations of the Framers of the Constitution and of the thinkers who influenced them with respect to legislative delegations of power? What were the expectations of the public that ratified the Constitution? Whatever the thinking of the past, was it ever realistic to expect a body like Congress to be a fit repository for decisions on politically difficult questions? Can Congress represent a pluralistic constituency and still transcend the serious political divisions of that constituency? Is it always bad for Congress to evade responsibility for decision through the use of broad delegations? May not Congress sometime serve the public interest more effectively through broad delegations than through clear policy choices? What principles should guide the agencies and the courts in responding to overly broad delegations? Should the courts prefer the risks of legislative inaction to delegations which carry hopes of at least some action by institutions other than Congress? Should the courts attempt to force

Congress into adequate levels of decision in all cases or only in those affecting values seen as constitutionally preferred? Do the agencies have special obligations to narrow the range of uncertainty under broad delegations by generating clear rules of their own? In structuring their own discretion under broad delegations should the agencies and the courts be guided by their own preferences, or should they instead attempt to discern and anticipate the will of Congress? These are only some of the questions we would have to confront in order to claim a full appreciation of the delegation problem as a whole.

The questions we ask in this study come from the remaining parts of the broader problem. We want to know whether the delegation doctrine is a genuine rule of the Constitution, its proper constitutional foundation and scope, and whether Congress can find constitutionally adequate substitutes. We would thus answer the general question: what minimal limitations on the power to delegate are reasonably implicit in the Constitution itself? Because we seek the least that the Constitution itself could mean, our concerns here are more narrowly legalistic than other aspects of the delegation problem. Our assumption is that other aspects of the problem typically arise after one has perceived a disjunction between law and actual practice. Entry to the delegation problem typically begins when one believes that the Constitution prohibits delegations but that Congress does and must continue to delegate. For this reason inquiry into the narrow, legal question of minimal constitutional meaning seems a useful starting point. What, indeed, is the least that the Constitution could reasonably mean for the practice of congressional delegations? Must it be understood to place any limits on delegation? If so, what and why? Through this inquiry we hope to make a limited contribution to an understanding of the broader problem of delegation.

The first issue confronted in Chapter 2 arises from the fact that no formulation of the delegation doctrine is an explicit part of the Constitution. This fact has enabled critics of the doctrine to deny that it has genuine constitutional status. We must therefore attempt to determine whether a rule of nondelegation is indeed an implicit part of the Constitution. Chapter 2 argues that a secure foundation for the rule can be found in the idea of constitutional supremacy, the idea that the Constitution with its arrangement of offices and powers is the supreme law of the land. The delegation doctrine has received different historical reformulations as it has been related over the years to a series of expanding delegations. The most modest kind of delegation, and the first to win approval of the Supreme Court, is that of power to "find and declare facts" on which the provisions of a statute would be applied. A seemingly more expansive kind of delegation is that of power to "fill in the details" of legislative enactments. A closely related type provides general statements of policy or "statutory standards" for the guidance of administrators, courts, and others. Still more expansive are delegations without statutory guidance. And the most expansive would be those adjudged abdications of power, with formal abdications defining the theoretical limits of these delegations. Because a prohibition against abdications seems implicit in the desire to establish and maintain a legally binding arrangement of offices and powers, this minimal function of the delegation doctrine seems firmly grounded in the idea of constitutional supremacy.

If the concept of constitutional supremacy supports the minimal function of prohibiting delegations adjudged abdications, what other doctrinal support might the delegation doctrine claim? To answer this question Chapter 2 turns to an investigation of the conceptual relationship between the delegation doctrine and the doctrines with which it has been most associated historically: the separation of powers, due process of law, and others. While these norms can be used to support the rule on different occasions, Chapter 2 argues that the best foundation for the rule lies in the idea of constitutional supremacy. For this reason it is argued further that the scope of the delegation doctrine need not extend beyond limits reasonably found in the idea of constitutional supremacy. Because Congress is prohibited from abdicating powers established by the Constitution as instruments for desired ends, it can be concluded that Congress should be governed by some idea of constitutional duty. It therefore seems reasonable to prohibit those delegations deliberately designed to evade responsibility for choice among alternatives most salient to Congress itself at the time of enactment. Delegation is thus proper whenever it appears instrumental to an exercise of power—that is, when it is put to the service of a choice among those most salient alternatives whose clashes constitute the most visible aspects of public debate. A delegation passing the burdens of such basic policy choices to others is more an abdication than an exercise of power. Such delegations should be held unconstitutional. Chapter 2 then develops a set of guidelines for applying this formulation of the rule to concrete cases. For example, those who apply the rule should concern themselves with evaluating the qualities of congressional decision and resolve; little is achieved by trying to determine whether the particular power delegated should be classified as "legislative," "executive," or in other terms associated with the separation of powers.

In Chapter 2 constitutional concepts are analyzed and their relationships explored in order to formulate general theories for later use as guides to the evaluation of concrete cases. This is attempted through reflection on the meaning of the Constitution from what we could term a prelitigational perspective, the perspective of one who seeks the law without specific controversies in mind and without a view to justifying particular political results. From this perspective we do not seek the meaning of the law to someone whom we identify as distinguished from others, we seek the meaning of the law to the typical reader of it, or, simply, we seek the meaning of the law itself. We assume, then, that it is possible for analyses of constitutional language to yield standards for the evaluation of cases, standards that are unbiased and nonpartisan, if not objective in all senses. To defend this assumption adequately would require a discussion too lengthy for an introduction to this essay on delegation. Moreover, one can hope that such a discussion would be unnecessary in view of the likelihood that few readers would deny the possibility of a dimension of constitutional meaning independent of the partisanship of those who read it. Nevertheless, some gesture, at least, to certain segments of the methodologically sensitive may be appropriate. In lieu of a full discussion, a few disclaimers in behalf of the present approach may suffice to lower a few barriers, if not to remove them altogether.

First, our approach does not assume either that the Constitution is free of indeterminate language or that the application of constitutional language is a mechanical process. Recognizing the indeterminateness and the discretionary aspects, we assert only that there are large areas of clarity in constitutional language which could limit the operations of government by providing limits to the discretion of those who apply constitutional rules. Second, we do not hold that institutional change must strictly conform to the expectations of those who write and ratify constitutions. But it appears reasonable that there are limits to legitimate change and that among the several sources of those limits are the meanings of the Constitution. Nor do we suggest that the search for constitutional meaning should exclude the deeper intentions of the Framers, their philosophic tradition, or the needs and thought of current and future generations. On the other hand, serious problems, theoretical and practical, seem to attend the practice of invoking deeper intentions and more pressing needs as justifications for ignoring or distorting the meaning of the document. Finally, we do not suggest opposition to the use of judicial cases in the study of constitutional doctrine. However, we would restore somewhat the distinction between the Constitution and its judicial gloss, and we would contend that a coherent account of events in judicial history requires principles which transcend the cases themselves. The meaning of the Constitution itself is one source of those principles, as are such other sources as the deeper intentions of the Framers and the needs of current generations.

Chapter 3 turns from theoretical discussion to evaluation of cases. The cases selected represent the principal phases of the delegation doctrine's judicial evolution and include most of the Supreme Court's leading delegation decisions. While these cases are discussed in historical order for the most part, and while the various approaches of the Court are compared with the one required by our analysis, Chapter 3 does not attempt to substitute a case law of our own for the Court's. We recognize, to begin with, that our approach is based on a theory of the least that the Constitution could imply about delegation, whereas the Court would have had the doctrine serve a broader range of values. We also recognize that the guidelines we employ permit a range of applications. The aim of Chapter 3 is rather to illustrate one observer's applications in order to show something of the questions which should be asked in evaluating delegation cases. Accordingly, we shall concentrate on problems of describing congressional resolve relative to policy alternatives of high salience to Congress at the time of enactment. On this basis we shall offer our evaluations of constitutionality. But the claims made for these evaluations center more on the questions raised than on the answers. The reader may feel that our answers tend to be permissive. However, the same kind of analysis could easily result in judgments significantly less permissive. The important thing from our perspective is that the Constitution requires that Congress be held to some meaningful standards of responsibility and choice; within limits, those standards may be applied differently by different observers.

Chapter 4 concludes the book with an effort to determine whether Congress can find substitutes for the delegation doctrine in the techniques of legislative oversight, as some students of the subject have suggested. These techniques include the appropriations process, the legislative investigation, and provisions for vetoing administrative decisions through action by both houses, either house, or committees of either house. If these techniques are constitutionally adequate substitutes for the delegation doctrine, as formulated here, then they can be evaluated in terms of their utility in helping Congress make policy after enactment of broad delegations. The analysis shows that the only device that comes close to satisfying the norms supporting the delegation doctrine is a statutory commitment to review and reenact statutes with overly broad delegations. These provisions typically take the form of limited periods of statutory duration. As we shall see, however, even mandatory review and reenactment is significantly less than perfect as a substitute for adherence to the delegation doctrine. One reason is the difficulty of legitimizing deprivations of life, liberty, and property under statutes conceived as experimental. Another is the prospect that experimental periods may sometimes end not in choices for Congress but in faits accomplis, as is particularly likely in limited delegations of the war power. If, in any event, there is any adequate substitute for abiding by the duty to decide, it is this commitment to decide eventually.

The rule of non-delegation: Its conceptual origins and properties

From an early point in our constitutional history to the present, the rule of nondelegation has generally been recognized by judges and commentators as a part of the Constitution. Nevertheless, the Constitution does not explicitly state that Congress may not delegate any or even all of its powers to others. What, then, are the constitutional concepts at the foundation of the delegation doctrine? Several principles have been cited over the years. The rule of nondelegation is most frequently labeled a corollary of the separation of powers doctrine. It has also been called an import into constitutional law from the common law of agency where an ancient maxim prohibits the redelegation of delegated power (*delegata potestas non potest delegari*). The rule of nondelegation has been seen as an invention of the courts, aimed at protecting the rule of law from the encroachments of discretionary authority. In this connection the rule of nondelegation has been construed as a corollary of the idea of due process of law. Sometimes the rule has been regarded as the result of what is believed to be a constitutional commitment to the legislature as the repository of popular trust, but other theorists have seen the rule as resting on principles of republican government which were instituted to overcome the precipitancy and incompetence of popular assemblies.

Because it is not mentioned explicitly in the Constitution and in view of this variety of sometimes conflicting principles at the supposed foundations of the rule of nondelegation, it is not surprising that some commentators have argued that the rule has no genuine constitutional status at all.

Kenneth Culp Davis has pursued the most successful attack, arguing that the nondelegation doctrine is "wholly judge-made," that it conflicts with the spirit of the necessary and proper clause,[1] that it fails to reflect the realities of the way modern courts actually handle delegations, and that it represents the simplistic idea that power can be divided "neatly once and for all between legislative and administrative authorities."[2] Patrick W. Duff and Horace E. Whiteside concluded their well-known study of the rule a generation ago by contending that the rule is not a legitimate principle of constitutional law. "There is no mention of it in any American constitution," they argued, "nor any remote reference to it. The whole doctrine, insofar as it is asserted to be a principle of constitutional law, is built upon the thinnest of implications, or it is the product of the unwritten superconstitution."[3] Others who have doubted the constitutional status of the rule include Rocco J. Tresolini,[4] Carl J. Friedrich,[5] John P. Roche,[6] and, when he was assistant attorney general, Robert H. Jackson.[7]

A natural starting point for a study of the rule of nondelegation is the problem of the rule's constitutional status, and this is the issue of central concern in this chapter. It would appear that the constitutional status of the rule could be established if it could be shown that the rule is implicit in principles whose authority in constitutional theory is beyond question. The primary purpose of this chapter is to make that showing.

In outline, the argument of this chapter is that a prohibition against those delegations which amount to abdications of power is a corollary of the idea of constitutional supremacy to be found in the expectations of people who organize institutions and vest them with powers of government. Although the rule of nondelegation is frequently linked with the separation of powers doctrine, the common-law maxim of agency, the idea of due process and the rule of law, and the concepts of representative democracy mentioned above, and although each of these doctrines may prohibit delegations on different occasions, an analysis of these doctrines shows that from a logical point of view the best theoretical foundation for the rule of nondelegation is the concept of constitutional supremacy. Once we have seen the weaknesses of the other concepts as theoretical foundations for the rule, the idea of constitutional supremacy will become for us the source of criteria for the rule's application to acts of Congress.

Among the influences against applying the principle of nondelegation to Congress is the feeling that, by applying the principle, we would risk depriving ourselves of much of the administrative process and, thereby, of the possibility of effective government in a modern society. This chapter will try to show that properly understood the rule of nondelegation is an essential rule of constitutionalism as defined in America. However, this chapter will also argue that in view of the values most clearly served by the rule of nondelegation, it is not necessary to give the term "delegation" the broad scope implicit in the comments of many who have criticized the courts for "legal fictions that what delegation is in fact is not delegation in law."[8] Formulated in terms of its proper values, the rule of nondelegation would indeed condition congressional use of the administrative process but not necessarily in all of the negative ways imagined by most of the rule's critics. This chapter closes with the suggestion that there may not be fundamental opposition between the idea of nondelegation, properly understood, and the needs of modern government.

The Minimal Function of the Rule of Nondelegation

The Preamble and Article VII tell us that certain groups of people ratified the Constitution for certain purposes, and, thus, that the Constitution has its genesis in a practical political proposal as a set of means for achieving certain desired ends. The ends of the Constitution ("justice," "domestic tranquility," and so on) are expressed on a rather high level of generalization, and Americans have always debated the institutional means to realizing these ends. In recent years, for example, we have asked ourselves the institutional question of how best to relate the war powers of Congress and the president for the sake of such ends as domestic tranquility and the common defense. Although disputes over institutional forms and relationships have frequently suggested that the institutional means to the ends of government are valued as ends in themselves, the knowledge that one generation of Americans was free to accept or reject our basic institutional framework has had its effect on the constitutional attitudes of subsequent generations. Knowing what we know about the freedom of the founding generation to accept or reject the Constitution, it has always seemed a little irrational to accept our institutions as ends in themselves—especially when a given arrangement appears to impede the kinds of moves thought necessary for desirable social results. From the beginning, an ends-orientation has remained a durable part of our constitutional character.

While an instrumental facet is clearly an essential feature of the Constitution, which originated in practical needs and proposals, the fact that the document was ordained and established as the "supreme law of the land" indicates that it cannot be adequately conceptualized as a mere set of means. Rules possessing only instrumental qualities are dependent for their authority solely on the values and perceptions of those to whom they are recommended. Such rules would not be rules of law. If there is no other reason to obey a rule than the desirable things it purports to achieve, then one is free to ignore the rule if one decides either that he does not want what the rule purports to bring about or that the desired result cannot actually be reached through the rule. As both "law" and "supreme law," however, the Constitution is more than a set of mere means which we are free to accept or reject on such grounds—its procedures are now presented as legally binding. The language of the Preamble and the provisions for ratification in Article VII tell us not only that the Constitution orginated in a practical political proposal submitted to an autonomous people, but also, when construed with the rule of constitutional supremacy in Article VI, that the founding generation intended to bind itself and subsequent generations to certain ways of doing the business of government. On its face, the Constitution is presented as law to be obeyed no matter what we feel about the ends it may serve or its utility in achieving them. To deny that the Constitution has this binding quality in some degree is to contend that there are no limitations on our freedom to change the Constitution.

It is true that one must assume the necessity for constitutional change, and this necessity is recognized in the amending provisions of Article V. But it is not true that the Constitution admits the possibility of unlimited constitutional change. For one thing, the amending provisions of Article V establish specific procedural criteria for the recognition of authoritative constitutional modifications. These procedures are themselves a limitation on constitutional change. Second, Article V indicates that even when conforming to authorized procedures, there are substantive limits to what can be done. After specifying the amending procedures, Article V provides a now obsolete prohibition of certain amendments which could have affected the taxation and importation of slaves prior to 1808. Article V also says that "no State, without its consent, shall be deprived of its equal suffrage in the Senate." Commenting on the theoretical significance of these limits, Corwin says:

> The amending, like all other powers organized in the Constitution, is in form a delegated, and hence a limited power . . . the one power known to the Constitution which clearly is not limited by it is that which ordains it—in other words, the original, inalienable power of the people of the United States to determine their own political institutions.[9]

Thus, by its own terms, as well as by the predominant understanding of a tradition, the Constitution as law represents an act designed in part to govern, limit, and restrict certain of the procedures of government.[10]

It thus appears that there is a logical conflict between the instrumental and the legal aspects of the Constitution, and that legalistic inflexibility must be characteristic of the Constitution at some level of abstraction. This conflict arises partly from the fact that institutional means conceived as fruitful under a given set of historical circumstances may not prove so under all circumstances. To the degree that conditions change, the procedures for achieving a set of ends are indeterminate. On this basis Hamilton cautioned in the twenty-third *Federalist* against encumbering the powers of the national government with limitations. "These powers ought to exist without limitations: *Because it is impossible to foresee or define the extent and variety of national exigencies, or the correspondent extent and variety of the means which may be necessary to satisfy them.*"[11] But even if we go to lengths Hamilton never reached and hold that the national government enjoys a general and undifferentiated power to govern in the national interest without effective exemptions in the form of individual rights, we would still be a great distance from a completely flexible constitution. Even if we were to forget about enumerating individual rights and governmental powers,[12] there would still be a need to organize or structure the government in accordance with rules of some sort, and however permissive these rules might be they would place *some* limits on governmental competence. The completely flexible, completely adaptive, constitution is more than just utopian, it is inconceivable.

Thus, at some level of abstraction at least, legalistic inflexibility is and must be a constitutional property. To some this inflexibility may represent the irrationality of elevating means over ends and the inequity of institutionalizing the superiority of the constitution-making generation over its posterity. But these injustices would be avoidable only if there were ways of perpetuating an operational consensus on the ends of government and eliminating the discrimination among competing values at the essence of political choice. Whatever else might be said about the logical conflict between the instrumental and legal aspects of the Constitution, those who write and ratify such rules must be understood to conceive of themselves as removing certain institutional alternatives from the sphere of legally uninhibited choice. Whatever the justification for their attitudes, those who write constitutions, then and now, intend that their constructs have some degree of prospective and binding effect. The same is true for those who ratify constitutions. It is only natural that from this attitude there should result an interest in maintaining the normative character of the arrangement of offices and powers ordained by the constitution-making authority.

In at least one of its applications—as a prohibition against the abdication of constitutionally imposed duties—the rule of nondelegation arises from this interest in maintaining the binding character of the constitutional arrangement of offices and powers. The history of the rule of nondelegation, as we shall see in Chapter 3, finds litigants, jurists, and commentators relating the doctrine to a series of overlapping and progressively expanding delegations of power, the most extreme of which end in abdication or delegations amounting to abdication. The narrowest and least problematic delegation is the power to "find and declare the facts" on which the operation or suspension of legislative policy is contingent. Congress, for example, might decide to declare that if and when a certain nation should engage in future hostile acts of a specified nature, an embargo should be placed upon its shipping. Congress could then delegate to the president the power to determine if and when the hostile acts had occurred; a presidential declaration to this effect would result in putting the embargo into operation. A more obvious degree of discretion is involved when Congress delegates the power to "fill up the details" of generally phrased legislative enactments. Thus, the courts might uphold a delegation to exclude from import unspecified "substandard grades of tea" on the grounds that the judgment required of the administrator was not "legislative" or "discretionary" in character but one of "filling up the details" of the authorizing statute. Closely following is the delegation of rulemaking power which the courts concede to be discretionary but which they find is accompanied by "legislative standards" as guides for administrators and reviewing courts. Next come delegations of discretionary authority without guiding standards, some fairly specific about the subjects to be regulated, some not. Some legislation, for example, may specify "railroads" as the subject of discretionary authority, while others may refer only to "industries engaged in interstate and foreign commerce." Delegations which are regarded broad enough to be labeled equivalent to abdications follow, and, finally, there would be abdication in the formal sense.[13]

We shall discuss the different kinds of delegations more fully in Chapter 3, but for the moment the least that can be said is that delegations of the most extreme kinds would defeat the desire to maintain the constitutional arrangement of offices and powers. This is so because abdication would be one of the ways of destroying the constitutional arrangement. If the desire to maintain the constitutional arrangement of offices and powers is expressed in the concept of constitutional supremacy, then the concept of constitutional supremacy can provide us with the origin of that application of the nondelegation doctrine which would prevent the abdication of constitutionally imposed duties. Why not abdication? Because abdication would result in a new arrangement of offices and powers. Why not a new arrangement? Because the old arrangement was established as supreme law by what is thought to be authority superior to all other legal authority. Consider the following passage on delegation from Locke's *Second Treatise* Section 141:

> . . . The legislative cannot transfer the power of making laws to any other hands; for it being but a delegated power from the people, they who have it cannot pass it over to others. The people

alone can appoint the form of the commonwealth, which is by
constituting the legislative and appointing in whose hands that
shall be. And when the people have said, we will submit to rules
and be governed by laws made by such men, and in such forms,
nobody else can say other men shall make laws for them; nor can
the people be bound by any laws but such as are enacted by those
whom they have chosen and authorized to make laws for them.
The power of the legislative, being derived from the people by a
positive voluntary grant and institution, can be no other than
what the positive grant conveyed, which being only to make laws,
and not to make legislators, the legislative can have no power to
transfer their authority of making laws and place it in other
hands.

We can see in this statement on the prohibition how it can be
grounded in the expectations of supreme authority, expectations
which perhaps would prohibit not only abdications, but even
delegations of more modest scope.

The minimal function of the rule of nondelegation would thus
appear to be the proscription of these extreme delegations which are
adjudged abdications of power.[14] Later in this chapter we shall
attend to the problems of relating these extreme delegations to
delegations of lesser scope. For the moment, however, we seek only
to establish the proposition that for at least one of the historical
senses of the word "delegation," namely, "abdication," the rule of
nondelegation is grounded in a concept of unquestionable constitutional status, the concept of constitutional supremacy.

As a norm prohibiting the abdication of congressional power,
there seems to be no successful way to deny that the rule of
nondelegation enjoys constitutional status. If it be objected that the
rule, even in its minimal scope, is not an explicit rule of the
Constitution, we need only note that the same can be said of a
number of constitutional norms, concepts, and practices, including
others aimed at maintaining constitutional supremacy.[15] Judicial
review as presented by Marshall,[16] executive prerogative as defended
by Lincoln,[17] federal supremacy as defended by Holmes[18]—each of
these doctrines has been presented as a barrier to practices which
would destroy the system, and the fact that they are not explicitly
sanctioned, while important, has proved of no conclusive significance. If it be argued that, even in its minimal scope, the rule of
nondelegation conflicts with a supposedly unlimited grant to Con-

gress of discretion over legislative means in the necessary and proper clause,[19] we need only reply that the necessary and proper clause by its own language is predicated on the existence of enumerated and specified powers possessed by other departments of the government *and by Congress,* and that it is a grant of power to exercise other powers, not to abdicate them.[20]

Should it be argued that Congress may abdicate if and to the extent that such action would further ends of government which Congress is no longer able or willing to pursue effectively, we can only repeat that neither ours nor any other constitution can be a completely ends-oriented instrument.[21] The Constitution does commit us to the pursuit of certain ends. But at some point it also makes the use of certain means mandatory. Among those means are the rules establishing Congress, staffing Congress, delimiting some of its relationships with other units of government, and granting substantive powers to a body so constituted and situated. For Congress to abandon those powers because it feels that it is ill-equipped to handle them or because it is unwilling to handle them on other grounds, is for Congress to substitute its judgment and desires for those expressed in the Constitution. There is no doubt that the judgment and desires of current Congresses may be superior in many respects to those of the founding generation—but there is also no doubt that there is a point at which we must consult more than current values and demands in order to determine the meaning of the Constitution.

A more formidable question arises, however, as to whether anything important follows from the seemingly trivial argument that the idea of constitutional supremacy is the source of that application of the rule of nondelegation which would prohibit the abdication of congressional powers and responsibilities. It can be objected that to find a constitutional foundation for the most modest and least problematic application of the rule proves nothing about the less modest and more problematic applications. After all, the delegation debate, historically, has concerned, not the continued existence of Congress as an effective institution, but the degree to which Congress may entrust large powers to executive, judicial, administrative, and private agencies.

The determination of whether and to what extent this objection is sound must await analysis below. However, several points can be made now as to the significance of the conclusion that the prohibition against the abdication of congressional power is grounded in the concept of constitutional supremacy. First, our argument implies that to deny that the rule of nondelegation has any constitutional status at all entails the conclusion that the power of Congress to delegate is completely unlimited, extending even to the point of total abdication. With one possible exception, not one of the delegation doctrine's critics has been willing to take this extreme position. Even Davis, the doctrine's best-known opponent, appears willing to grant that the power to delegate has limits significantly short of abdication.[22] Few of the rule's other critics would attempt to deny this modest limit on the power to delegate. However, one commentator, John Roche, has appeared willing to assert the logical consequence of the premise that the power to delegate is constitutionally unlimited.

Roche has written that

the notion that delegated power cannot be further delegated has been demolished by constitutional logic drawn from John Marshall: that congressional power where it exists is plenary, and that plenary jurisdiction includes the power to give power away. Limits on delegation do exist, but they are political, not constitutional in character.[23]

This is not the place to examine Roche's interpretation of what Marshall did say about the scope of congressional power where it exists. But it must be said that Marshall refused to draw from what he did say about the scope of congressional power an explicit conclusion that plenary jurisdiction includes the power to give power away.

As we shall see in Chapter 3, Marshall's statement on our subject is subtle and provocative, and, indeed, it may well imply an argument which could support the constitutionality of congressional abdication or something close to it.[24] However, it is a matter of substantial significance that Marshall is generally regarded as having decided that congressional power to delegate extended only to the "details" of legislative decisions and that Congress could not delegate its power over important legislative matters.[25] We shall see that Marshall may have held the most permissive theory of delegation of any American jurist—but Marshall's permissive theory, even if it does exist, is well hidden by language which is clearly designed to communicate the theory that Congress may delegate power over details only. Whatever Marshall's hidden theory, the fact is that he has been received as having enunciated a restrictive theory, and it is patent on the surface of his remarks that he intended to be received as he has been received.[26] The point here, however, is not that Roche is wrong about what he may impute to Marshall, but that, in view of the way Marshall has been generally received, the burden falls on Roche to show that Marshall really meant to say something else. As it stands, we are entitled to say that Marshall has publicly disagreed with the proposition that the power to delegate is without constitutional limitations.

However, Roche does not actually say that Marshall said that plenary jurisdiction includes the power to give power away. Roche says rather that this conclusion can be established by an argument "drawn from" Marshall. At that point Roche refers his readers to a thirty-four page article on the subject of executive prerogative in domestic emergency written by Roche himself.[27] Early in his article he states that

> most of the President's powers in domestic emergencies have grown out of congressional delegations of power. Nevertheless, there seems to be little point to an elaborate examination of these delegated powers because there are no existent criteria of limitation. In fact, when the President and Congress coordinately and cooperatively recognize the existence of an emergency, there appear to be no limits to the power that the legislature can constitutionally confer upon the executive to cope with the problem.[28]

He cites the Japanese-American "relocation" during World War II and the Court's decision in the *Korematsu* case as an example.[29] Later he states that the Court will "rarely if ever frustrate the exercise of real political power," that "real political power normally is shared between the President and Congress," and that "however the process of adjustment may be justified, the Constitution will be found flexible enough to authorize almost any conceivable congressional delegation of emergency power to the executive."[30] With this comment Roche excludes from his inquiry into executive prerogative that portion of executive power which results directly from congressional delegations. And this appears to be the extent of the support for his argument that "plenary jurisdiction includes power to give power away."

Roche's observations may lead to a normative conclusion as far as he is concerned, but from the perspective here there is simply no necessary connection between the premise that the Court will accept any degree of delegation and the conclusion that the legal *power* to delegate is unlimited. From a legalistic perspective the nature and extent of congressional power depends on what the Constitution has authorized, not on what Congress can get away with—even with the help of the Court. Roche's argument reflects an understanding of the Constitution as a document capable of unlimited growth and adaptability, an understanding we have rejected here.[31] Perhaps the Court has expanded a power to declare facts and fill up details into a power to abdicate power altogether, but that is a historical proposition, not a legal one.

If it is untenable that the Constitution possesses unlimited flexibility and adaptability, however, it is equally implausible that its concepts are capable of no flexibility whatever. For example, it is easy to see how a power to delegate the filling up of details could develop into a power to confer rule-making authority under the guidance of statutory standards which reflect legislative decision among relatively general policy alternatives. Filling up details implies what Pritchett has called "an announced general legislative plan into which the details fit," and from this implication the requirement of legislative standards has evolved.[32] On the other hand, it is difficult to see how the logic of "filling up details" could sanction delegations in the absence of announced general legislative plans, and it is very difficult if not impossible to see how a power to fill up details—implying as it does an announced general legislative plan into which the details fit—can imply a power to abandon jurisdiction altogether.

With the observation that constitutional concepts exhibit limited adaptibility, we come to a second reason for supposing that something of practical importance may follow from the argument that the Constitution prohibits the abdication of congressional power. As the relatively trivial power to delegate the filling up of details has expanded to increasingly permissive limits—even to a power to delegate without standards and beyond—so may a rule against abdication easily expand in another direction. Most if not all of the commentators who employ the term "abdication" in the context of the delegation question recognize clearly that Congress need not give power away in a total, formal, and irretrievable way before the word "abdication" is appropriate.[33] The rule of nondelgation need not be confined only to abdications of a formal nature. The same values making the rule applicable to formal abdications prohibit delegations so broad as to be reasonably judged as "amounting to abdications." And who is to say that the values prohibiting abdication preclude a concept of abdication broad enough to embrace those delegations not accompanied by "an announced general plan"? The degree to which the minimal application of our rule may be expanded remains to be seen. But surely few could deny that it is far more reasonable to expand a rule prohibiting abdications to one prohibiting delegations without meaningful statutory standards than it has been to expand a rule permitting the delegation of details to one permitting delegations without any standards at all.

Nondelegation and Its Historical Associations

We turn now to the task of relating the rule of nondelegation to those other constitutional norms with which history has associated it: the separation of powers, the common-law maxim of agency, the idea of due process, the legislature as repository of popular trust, and the idea of republican government. In pointing out why and in what respects the rule should be separated from these other norms, the way is prepared for a clear focus on those considerations which yield sound criteria for the rule's application to acts of Congress. Our investigation will show that while the scope of the rule can be extended greatly when based upon norms other than that of constitutional supremacy, and while these other norms can support the rule on different occasions, none of these other norms provides a satisfactory logical foundation for the rule. On this basis we shall conclude that the criteria for the rule's proper application are to be derived from the concept of constitutional supremacy and, therefore, that the scope of the rule need not extend beyond limits imposed by that concept.

As our discussion progresses the reader may come to feel that concepts which have been traditionally understood as corollaries are being artificially separated here. We shall distinguish, for example, some of the abstract organizational aspects of separation of powers and representative government from those expectations which have traditionally rendered them legally binding as systems of constitutional law. We must hope that justifications for these logical distinctions will be found in what we have already said about the limitations of our analysis and in the quality of the analysis itself. To summarize earlier caveats, we seek to explicate only a rather narrow, legalistic aspect of a problem which cannot be fully understood without a broader inquiry than the present one. We also point out that the delegation doctrine's historical associations have not been strong enough to save it from its current desuetude. In the face of that desuetude we seek the doctrine's strongest foundation, not necessarily its only one. And if that means we have to settle for the doctrine's minimal scope, such may be the price of our search.

The Separation of Powers

The rule of nondelegation is more frequently and regularly associated with the separation of powers than it is with any other concept. Robert E. Cushman speaks for most of the commentators when he terms the idea of nondelegation as a "corollary of the doctrine of the separation of powers."[34] There would be no point in upsetting this widely held view if it were not for the resulting tendency to think that nondelegation applies either because power is separated or because power is specified as legislative, executive, judicial, and so on.[35] The separation and specification of power determine the substantive content of the prohibition, to be sure, but the basic reason for the rule is to be found in the fact that power has been granted or vested by higher authority, not in the fact that power has been specified and separated. More generally put, the rule of nondelegation derives from the expectations peculiar to the act of granting power and not from the organizational specifics which comprise the content of the grant.

Before discussing why it may be useful to separate the delegation doctrine from the separation of powers, let us satisfy ourselves that such a separation is possible. To begin with, the idea of nondelegation seems more fundamental than the separation of powers. That the powers of government are delegated by the people in an arrangement binding on the government seems more fundamental than the specifics of that arrangement. Certainly the idea of nondelegation does not necessarily imply the idea of separated powers, as is indicated by the rule of nondelegation in the common law of agency, a rule that does not depend on how the agent's power is structured.[36] Moreover, the separation of powers is itself an implied norm of the Constitution, and one partly dependent on a principle of nondelegation. True, power is divided in some measure, but whether it ought to remain divided depends partly on whether an expectation of nondelegation attaches to the division. This expectation typically accompanies a grant of power, but it does not have to, and it may be defeated by a simple declaration that delegations are permissible. A case in point is the Constitution of the Fifth Republic, a provision of which empowers the executive to request delegations in matters reserved to parliament.[37] In principle, granted power may not be delegated beyond constitutional provisions whether that power is in any sense divided or not, and when power is divided there is nothing to prevent provisions for delegating. Finally, nondelegation could not follow simply because the power in question is "legislative." If it did, then the delegation of that power to the government by the people could not have taken place in the first place, a delegation attested to by history, political philosophy, and the Constitution itself.[38]

Given that it is logically possible to separate the rule of nondelegation from the separation of powers principle, it is a useful separation for at least two reasons. First, the independence of nondelegation from separation of powers is of material significance for the effort to state the conditions under which the former applies to acts of Congress. If nondelegation originates in a particular act of granting power, then it is to be applied to certain kinds of congressional acts, not because congressional power is legislative in nature or because it is separated from other kinds of power, but because it is power which has been granted by a higher authority.[39] Nondelegation applies because the power in question is *granted*—not because it is either *legislative* or *separated*. It would appear to follow from this that the rule should not be invoked merely because congressional action (or inaction) results in rule-making by units other than Congress, nor should it be invoked merely because congressional action results in a merging of legislative, executive, and judicial functions on administrative and other noncongressional levels, or even because congressional action results in greater fragmentations of power than existed in the first place. Instead of looking to the theoretical and practical problems of distinguishing and blending the several powers of government, we might better determine when to apply the rule by looking to the expectations of people when they grant power. As we shall see, this approach will permit the application of the rule to be conditioned less by qualities of agency organization and decision and more by qualities of congressional decision among competing policy alternatives.

The second reason for maintaining a line between nondelegation and the separation of powers is to impose new burdens on some of those who would weaken the former through attacks on the latter. An argument against the rule of nondelegation is theoretically inadequate if its sole basis is the view that, unaided by the administrative component, Congress is incapable of handling modern problems. As an attack on nondelegation, this view presupposes that the rule is a corollary of the separation of powers and with it an obstacle to the development of the administrative process. Properly understood, the rule is more than a corollary of the separation of powers, and, as we shall see, it need not be applied to forbid extensive congressional use of the administrative process. Eventually it will appear that in order to undermine successfully the rule of nondelegation one would have to attack the legalistic renditions of constitutional supremacy discussed above and argue that constitutionalism itself can no longer be understood as it was in the tradition. It may or may not be possible ultimately to conclude that the activities of organizing governments, granting them powers, and limiting their exercise are futile efforts to do the impracticable, but that will be the only argument on which a total rejection of nondelegation can be based.

Delegata Potestas Non Potest Delegari

Frequently cited in connection with the rule of nondelegation is the common-law maxim *delegata potestas non potest delegari,* which can be translated to read that power which is originally delegated may not be redelegated. This maxim is seen in the literature primarily as a maxim of the common law of agency, although some commentators treat it as a rule of constitutional law as well. For purposes of clarity in this part of our discussion, let us distinguish between (1) the common-law maxim of agency, as presented above, (2) the rule of American constitutional law prohibiting the delegation of congressional power, that is, the "rule of nondelegation," and (3) the general principle of nondelegation which attaches to any delegated power from superior authority unaccompanied by expressed provisions to the contrary, whether that power be legislative or other, in the law of agency, in constitutional law, or elsewhere.

Obviously these norms are closely related, and the first two appear to be mere applications of the third in specified areas. By distinguishing them we avoid the erroneous conclusion, to be discussed, that the rule of American constitutional law is weakened by findings of misinterpretations of, and corruptions in, the texts of common-law authorities.

It might be desirable to treat the common-law maxim as the source of the rule of American constitutional law for at least two reasons. First, the rule prohibiting the delegation of legislative power is not an explicit rule of the Constitution, and, we have seen, some of its opponents are quick to point this out in an effort to deny the rule constitutional status. One surely recovers some of this status by tying the rule to a maxim honored in the common law before and since Bracton and Coke. Secondly, and more importantly for present purposes, the common-law maxim that *delegated* power cannot be redelegated more accurately directs explanations of the rule to expectations in the act of granting power and away from considerations more immediately relevant to the separation of powers. Thus, the common-law maxim is a better tool for understanding the basis for the rule of nondelegation than the separation of powers doctrine.

Notwithstanding these advantages, however, the close relationship between the common-law maxim and the rule of constitutional law has invited several related errors to the detriment of the latter. First, it encourages a case method of analysis which would explain the rule by concentrating on the judicial events in the rule's common-law history at the expense of commonsense expectations which clearly antedate the rule as dictum. Second, it fosters the view that the rule is entirely judge-made law. Finally, it is responsible for the idea that the rule of constitutional law is in some sense an import from the law of agency, and not fully authoritative on that account. These errors are visible in one of the most influential and respected statements in the literature of nondelegability, that of Duff and Whiteside on the common-law maxim as a rule of constitutional law.[40]

Duff and Whiteside attempt to show how the common-law maxim "came into existence" by tracing its "little known" history first to Coke and then to Bracton. They attempt to show that the formulations of neither of these authorities are sufficient to support the restrictions on legislative power threatened by the use of the maxim in American constitutional law. They do this by arguing that Coke's formulation applies only to delegations of jurisdiction and that Bracton's formulation, reinterpreted in light of a better manuscript, actually permits delegations so long as the delegating authority retains "the primary (or regulating) power."[41]

Upon reviewing the maxim's history and concluding that its "true scope" has been misunderstood, Duff and Whiteside turn to other norms supporting the constitutional rule, namely, the separation of powers and some of the ideas of representative democracy. The authors depreciate these norms variously as "inconvenient" political doctrines and "outworn concepts of the eighteenth century which have become the heritage of the nineteenth century demagogue," and find, in any event, that they are too vague to provide the law with certainty in the form of a fixed rule of decision.[42] They find that while appearing mostly as dictum when these other norms are discussed in the cases, the fixed rule of decision in the cases seems to be the common-law maxim. "The truth of the matter seems to be," they conclude,

> that Lord Coke's maxim, kept alive by discussion and *dicta* in the earlier cases, rises as a ghost to hamper the efficient and proper distributions of the functions of government. . . . The whole doctrine, insofar as it is asserted to be a principle of constitutional law, is built upon the thinnest of implications, or it is the product of the unwritten superconstitution.[43]

The first point that must be challenged in the Duff and Whiteside argument is the view that the only proper foundation for the constitutional rule is the common-law maxim. Surely the most plausible view is that the common-law maxim and the constitutional rule both express the same thought, but do so in different areas of the law. Neither of the more specific rules is grounded in the other; both express the more general principle that delegated power should not be redelegated, whether in agency or constitutional law or elsewhere. That there is a viable general principle of nondelegation is evident, as closer inspection will show, even in our authors' own conclusions. In their correction of Bracton's version of the maxim, for example, one is brought from the allegedly corrupt version that "delegated jurisdiction cannot be delegated" to the improved version that "jurisdiction cannot be delegated in such a manner that the jurisdiction (or power of regulating it) does not remain with the

King himself."[44] It is difficult to appreciate their conclusion that the second version "has annihilated" the first. To be sure, the new reading permits a greater latitude for delegation than the old, but the new reading is hardly intelligible in the absence of the assumption that at some point there is and ought to be a limit to permissible delegations.

Duff and Whiteside themselves indicate what the limit might be with the remark that they do "not wish to be understood as asserting that there is no constitutional principle under which the legislature can be prevented from repudiating its responsibility entirely or abdicating in favor of some other department or person."[45] With some confusion they admit that abdication is within the maxim's "proper field of operation."[46] The maxim is also said to be applied properly in delegations of jurisdiction and in the "discretionary acts of a true agent."[47] These concessions that the maxim has some applications are significantly underplayed, and in the end we are left without clear answers to questions which seem rather crucial for an essay which argues that the rule of nondelegation is "built upon the thinnest of implications." Just what is the principle which prevents the legislature from repudiating its responsibility entirely? How extensive must such repudiation be before one reaches the point of abdication? If the common-law maxim applies to a true agent, on what basis does it do so? Does this basis differ from that which makes it applicable to delegations of jurisdiction? Why should it be applicable to delegations of "jurisdiction" and not to delegations of legislative power? Is not any delegation of rule-making power a delegation of jurisdiction in some sense and to some degree? Why should the maxim be applicable to delegations of a "true agent" and not to delegations of congressional power? Is it a theoretical error to understand Congress as an "agent" of the people in whose name the Constitution was written?

Because our authors fail to give these questions adequate attention they have been widely interpreted as contending that the whole doctrine of nondelegation stems from a dubious copy of a medieval manuscript. This interpretation may not be fair to Duff and Whiteside. They do suggest a limit on delegations, and they do mention such broader norms as the separation of powers and ideas of representative government. Nevertheless, the prohibition against abdications receives little comment, and our authors give little evidence of recognizing that the broader norms can generate rules of law in their own right. Because Duff and Whiteside offer no good reasons for rejecting these other norms, their critics have held their findings on the common-law maxim an insufficient basis for denying constitutional status to the delegation doctrine. Horst P. Ehmke argues that the rule can be grounded in Locke's doctrine of consent and the consent-trust relationship between the people and their legislature,[48] and Jaffe believes that "the judges have . . . merely seized on a convenient legal formula to express the underlying thought of Locke that 'the legislature neither must nor can transfer the power of making laws to anybody else, or place it anywhere but where the people have.' "[49] Jaffe dismisses the Duff and Whiteside thesis by remarking that the idea of nondelegation

> would seem as aptly to rest on the notion of the truly represen-
> tative and functional character of the legislature, as on the
> legal maxim. If it be thought that the judges were reading the
> "vesting" provision itself, pursuant to the maxim, it may be
> replied that a maxim enforced by Coke, Story, and Kent over the
> course of 400 years is far more relevant to the interpretation
> of a modern document than an unknown reading of a thirteenth
> century text. And it would still seem to be the law that powers
> entrusted to an agent because of his special fitness to perform
> them are not delegable.[50]

Due Process of Law

Before turning to the suggestion that nondelegation is grounded in the consent-trust relationship between the people and their repesen- tatives, let us examine the logical connections between the concepts of nondelegation and due process of law. The connections between the two concepts can be shown to be either adventitious or reducible to that between nondelegation and the idea of the representative legislature suggested by Jaffe and Ehmke.

In commenting on the flexibility of the English constitution when handling "bullion" as "malleable" as the notion of due process, Rodney L. Mott remarks that "the standard acquired some new meaning with each important constitutional crisis in the develop- ment of individual liberty, and more than any other protection . . . was invoked by those who felt their rights threatened, and with each successive exercise of this arm of liberty it gained both in effective- ness and ultimate potential value."[51] But Mott's recognition and approval of such malleability does not prevent him from expressing surprise that someone could conceive the idea of due process as proscribing the delegation of legislative power to regulatory commissions.[52] John D. McGowen is another writer who fails to see a conceptual link between the ideas of due process and nondelegation, finding instead a mere historical connection brought about by an old judicial commitment to laissez-faire. As McGowen understands it, "if a statute wrongfully delegated legislative power, it probably interfered with certain of the individual liberties that were deemed protected by the due process clause. Hence it frequently happened that the person who felt himself aggrieved by administrative action would challenge the statute under which the action was taken as being in violation of the due process clause as well as on the ground that it contained an unwarranted delegation of legislative power. State statutes could be challenged in federal courts only in this manner.[53] Hence the two doctrines tended to merge into one."[54]

While there may not be a strict conceptual link between nondelegation and due process, Cushman offers an explanation which appears to reveal a more substantial connection than the one noted by McGowan. Cushman explains the connection as follows:

> It is hard to escape the conviction that the rule against the
> delegation of legislative power, like the rule against the merger
> of the three powers of government in the same hands, is likely to
> be assimilated into the constitutional guarantee of due process
> of law. The delegations of legislative power which the courts
> have held bad are those in which legislative power has been
> given to executive or administrative officers without the pro-
> tection of a guiding standard, a standard which not only serves
> to direct the officer exercising the power but which enables a
> reviewing court to decide whether he has followed that guidance.
> There is an important practical reason for this rule. It is for
> the protection of the rights of the citizens that democratic
> governments vest the exercise of broad and untrammeled legisla-
> tive discretion in a representative legislature, and not in a
> single officer or agency. To permit such an officer or agency
> to exercise legislative power without the restraining influences
> of legislative "standards" is to subject the citizen to the danger
> of an arbitrary power against which he may have no very effective
> protection. It is but a short step from this to the position that
> one whose rights have been adversely affected by the exercise of
> unrestrained legislative discretion in the hands of an administra-
> tive officer or agency is actually being deprived of liberty without

due process of law. In short, the effective rule against the delegation of legislative power as that rule is now construed exists not for the purpose of keeping alive an abstract principle of political philosophy but for the purpose of surrounding private rights with a protection just as easily and logically available under the due process clause. In fact, the doctrine of the non-delegability of legislative power could safely be scrapped as long as due process of law remains the effective constitutional guarantee it now is.[55]

In evaluating Cushman's statement several points are in order. First, although the nondelegation doctrine may have been used as a means of preventing denials of due process resulting from unrestrained discretion, it should not be assumed that due-process safeguards in the form of legal standards must issue from legislatures alone. Davis has recently argued that the traditional proposal for limiting discretionary power through requirements of meaningful statutory standards has proved "unpromising,"[56] and that the hope lies "not in better statutory standards, but in earlier and more elaborate administrative rule-making and in better structuring and checking of discretionary power" largely by the agencies themselves.[57] The point for our purposes is that broad delegations of discretionary authority do not eliminate the possibility of giving legal specificity to orders governing individual conduct. After the legislature has delegated broadly, the administrative delegatees may themselves develop specific rules of law to apply to individual conduct. If the principal matter at issue in the due-process claim involves the distinction between governing individual conduct by discretion and by rule, the simple answer is that rules formulated by administrators may be at least as good, *qua rules,* as those drafted by legislators.[58] The rule of nondelegation is linked with due process through the norm that individual conduct ought to be governed by rules only if the legislature alone is adequate to the task of making rules.

We note, second, Cushman's observation that the modern delegation doctrine aims not at "keeping alive an abstract principle of political philosophy" but at the protection of private rights. This indicates a substantive link between nondelegation and due process in addition to the link between nondelegation and the issue of administrative discretion. Understood in this way, the delegation doctrine aims at more than discretion as such, it aims at discretion whose exercise threatens private rights. We have noted McGowen's observation that this use of the delegation doctrine originated with the courts in an era of hostility to economic regulation. The modern Court also has invalidated or restricted by construction a number of overly broad legal standards that have resulted in threats to substantive civil liberties. Among the many examples is a municipal ordinance vesting broad licensing powers over the right to hold religious meetings on the streets,[59] a state law making a misdemeanor the use of "opprobrious words or abusive language tending to cause a breach of the peace,"[60] and a congressional act (to be discussed in Chapter 3), vesting broad discretionary powers over the issuance of passports.[61] The decisions in cases of this type have not been grounded in the delegation doctrine because it is not the delegations that are really at issue. The Court seeks to confine discretion in these cases in order to protect substantive rights. The point of confining discretion is to remove the threat to such rights, not to force lawmakers to assume responsibility for their violation. Nevertheless, because the Court's desire to limit discretion is a feature of such decisions, they have been interpreted as partial revivals of the delegation doctrine.[62]

The difficulty with grounding the delegation doctrine in substantive rights is that the objection to such delegations would not be the fact of delegation as such but the resulting injury to substantive rights. If substantive due process were the sole foundation of the rule of nondelegation, no delegation could be unconstitutional, however extreme, in the absence of injury to protected rights. Obviously, we cannot assume that all delegations would result in abridgment of protected rights. Congress may as readily protect substantive rights through broad delegations as injure them. Broad delegations in recent years to the federal courts and other agencies in the areas of minority rights and environmental protection reinforce Jaffe's observation that delegation is "the logical instrument of a 'forward' party if" sympathetic administration may develop the "tendency of a policy more aggressively than would the legislators."[63] It appears, therefore, that the only way the rule of nondelegation could consistently apply to congressional delegations affecting substantive rights is on the assumption that Congress alone is capable of protecting those rights.

Cushman's statement about the connections between due process and nondelegation thus expresses a special view of legislative competence: only a "representative legislature" can be entrusted with untrammeled discretion to make rules governing individual conduct and affecting individual rights. The proposition that due process is the source of nondelegation is reduced to the thought, suggested above by Jaffe and Ehmke, that the delegation doctrine expresses a democratic commitment to lawmaking by representative assemblies.

The Representative Principle

Is the rule of nondelegation rooted in the value of government by "representative" assemblies? An answer to this question might be thought to depend on the particular set of principles of representation ordained by the Constitution. But a lengthy inquiry into this complex subject is not needed for our purposes. Whatever philosophy of representation one might select, it could not be the foundation of the delegation doctrine unless it were accompanied by a rule of legalistic inflexibility like the one expressed in the principle of constitutional supremacy. This would be true of any principle of representation. If, for example, the Constitution were thought to ordain a representative system representative of constituency desires, Congress would be free to delegate without limit to the constituency itself unless prohibited from doing so by some legal norm independent of constituency desires. Thus, on a determination that the constituency is better representative of its own desires than Congress itself, Congress could delegate freely to private groups within the constituency or to the constituency as a whole. If, on the other hand, the proper system should be one representative of substantive ideals and standards whose value does not depend on constituency desires, then, unless prohibited by other rules, transfers of power as needed to serve these values would be permissible, perhaps obligatory. Congress, for example, might well decide that meaningful racial integration of public education is essential to the service of fundamental constitutional aspirations, regardless of public opinion to the contrary. Congress could then delegate in the form of vague statutory standards the power to achieve integration to agencies better insulated from public opinion, like the executive departments and the courts.

We have seen that in their challenges to the thesis of Duff and Whiteside both Jaffe and Ehmke argue that nondelegation can be based on the concept of the legislature as most representative of interests in the public and most worthy of popular trust on that account. Both writers cite Locke as the authority for the rule, as did Cooley before them.[64] We have already quoted the principal passage in the *Second Treatise,* a passage which affirms the people as the source of the government's delegated powers, concluding that

> The power of the legislative, being derived from the people by a positive voluntary grant and institution, can be no other than what that positive grant conveyed, which being only to make laws, and not to make legislators, the legislative can have no power to transfer their authority of making laws and place it in other hands.[65]

It is likely that those who cite this passage in support of the delegation doctrine construe as corollaries in this context concepts we are distinguishing: the idea of representation and the principle rendering a given system of representation binding as law. We call attention to the distinction simply because it is not enough to say that the value of representation, however defined, is a sufficient basis for a rule of nondelegation. Like the separation of powers, a given conception of representative government must be accompanied by a rule of constitutional supremacy—a rule giving binding legal status to the system in question.

We can see further that a value of representation would not be enough by considering a standard rejoinder to attacks on the administrative process as failing to insure that rules "be formulated in a democratic and representative atmosphere."[66] To such attacks Peter Woll has responded, "The administrative branch is highly representative, and it may be argued that it is more representative than Congress.... Given the greater access of these [private pressure] groups to the bureaucracy, constitutional representation of groups today is perhaps better achieved through the administrative process than in Congress, which is a state-oriented body."[67] On this basis one might easily accept delegations to state agencies, private groups, and electoral constituencies. However, such delegations would not be acceptable to all theories of representation, and certainly not to what has been called the "republican" principle that values be served which may exist independently of the narrow, partial interests which frequently predominate in popular assemblies. The republican theory would thus reject delegations "downward" to the constituency.[68] Yet, it might well approve delegations "upward" to the executive, the courts, and others better constituted than Congress for the pursuit of preferred ends.[69]

A system of representation is necessarily conceived as representing a set of persons or values. As with other instruments for achieving certain ends, procedural or substantive, conditions may arise under which it can no longer do the job it was designed to do. Congress could thus cease to be representative of whatever values or persons it is supposed to represent. If all that ground the delegation doctrine are the values of a given system of representation, delegations are justified when those values would be served better through institutions other than those in which power was originally vested. Doctrines of representation are incompatible with delegations of power only when additional doctrines render systems of representation legally binding irrespective of their success in serving the values which brought them forth.

The Proper Tenor and Scope of the Rule

The separation of powers, the common-law maxim of agency, the ideas of due process and the rule of law, the legislature as repository of popular trust, and the idea of republican representation—each of these norms sometimes can supply a measure of support for the rule of nondelegation. But each in turn brings values and problems which serve at other times to weaken the rule. The lines defining the concepts of "legislative," "executive," "judicial," and "administrative" power are difficult to describe, and, in any case, the Founders deliberately and openly rejected the strict separation of powers. The common-law origins and formulations of the maxim in the law of agency are uncertain and variable. The standards and rules which are requisites of due process need not be supplied by legislators alone. The consent-trust version of the representative principle is not incompatible with delegations downward, and the republican-government theory is not incompatible with delegations upward.

Our analysis shows, moreover, that none of these doctrines can provide the rule of nondelegation with an adequate logical foundation. While expressing the same thought in different areas of law, the rule of nondelegation and the common-law maxim of agency do not derive from each other. No necessary connection is apparent between the value of governing individual conduct by general and stable rules of law and the question of who retains or transfers the power to formulate such rules. Unless there is a requirement for preserving a given system of representation, delegations can be justified by the very values which the system was designed to serve. The nondelegability of congressional power does not seem implicit in the fact that it is termed "legislative power," or in the fact that the power of government is separated in some sense. And, by abstracting from the separation of powers the expectation that the particular arrangement of power will be preserved, we see that a principle of nondelegation is a presupposition of the separation of powers, not a rule derived from the separation of powers.

Thus, we are brought to the conclusion that the best theoretical foundation for the rule of nondelegation is the simple expectation in the constituent act of establishing government that neither the government nor any of its parts should change the constitutional arrangement of offices and powers. This expectation is given legal expression in the doctrine of constitutional supremacy. Because the Constitution has specified a certain arrangement of offices and powers, and because the Constitution is the supreme law, Congress may not substitute its will for the will of the constituent authority by destroying the constitutional arrangement through abdications. Efforts to define the scope of the rule of nondelegation and to bring the concept closer to operational meaning should be guided primarily by expectations expressed in the idea of constitutional supremacy, not by considerations uniquely associated with the separation of powers, the common-law maxim, the rule of law, and various philosophies of representation.

If we hold that the proper theoretical foundation for the rule of nondelegation is the concept of constitutional supremacy, it follows that the only use of the rule beyond legitimate controversy is the prohibition against abdications of power. But even with agreement on this general rule there would still be legitimate disagreement over what, precisely, constitutes delegations amounting to abdication. Before considering this problem, let us examine further the implications of the nondelegation doctrine as grounded in the concept of constitutional supremacy. We shall see that among the expectations in the act of establishing the Constitution is the notion that the government and its parts, including Congress, have a *duty* to perform the functions and powers entrusted to them. The idea that Congress has a duty to perform its functions will provide some help in developing guidelines for applying the delegation doctrine to acts of Congress.

The proposition that the Constitution imposes a duty on Congress to perform its functions arises from the conjunction of the document's instrumental and legal aspects. We have already seen that the Constitution has its genesis in a practical political proposal and that, by its own language, it is an instrument for the pursuit of certain ends. Moreover, we have argued that the concept of constitutional supremacy prohibits the abdication of constitutional powers. From the perspective of the officeholder, to be told that one may not abdicate power vested for purposes of pursuing certain ends is to be told that one may not evade the obligations and responsibilities of that pursuit. If Congress is prohibited from abdicating its powers, and if these powers are instruments for pursuing certain ends, it would appear that Congress has a duty to exercise these powers. The essential act in exercising these powers is deciding between conflicting proposals presented by clashing interests. And it would seem a reasonable and modest conclusion that Congress evades its constitutional obligations when it deliberately transfers to others the responsibility for decision among what public debate shows to be the most salient policy alternatives presented to it. If so, any such transfer may reasonably be pronounced an unconstitutional delegation of power. Let us elaborate this argument by considering some of the more obvious objections to it.

First, it can be argued that while the Constitution grants to Congress powers over specified areas of social life, in no part of the document is it stated that Congress has a *duty* to exercise those powers in any degree whatever.[70] It might as easily be contended that Congress has a duty to transfer its powers when it feels that others are better equipped to exercise them in the public interest. To this objection we can say that if Congress has a duty to transfer its powers under any circumstances, this duty is certainly not explicit in the document, and it is difficult to see how it could be made compatible with the idea that Congress is not free to alter the constitutional arrangement of offices and powers. On the other hand, that Congress has a duty to exercise its powers to some degree can be defended despite the fact that the duty is not explicitly set forth, and without offending other constitutional norms.

Our proposition, again, can claim at least a superficial plausibility: if Congress may not abdicate its powers, it has a duty to exercise them. The fact that this duty is not explicit can be explained rather simply as an indication that the Framers assumed that legislative power was of "an encroaching nature"[71] and that, therefore, there was no need to mandate its exercise. In introducing the system of checks and balances as a set of rules for maintaining among the departments of government "the degree of separation . . . essential to a free government," Madison said that, in addition to "parchment barriers,"

> . . . some more adequate defense is indispensibly necessary for the more feeble, against the more powerful members of the government. The legislative department is everywhere extending the sphere of its activity, and drawing all power into its impetuous vortex.
>
> The founders of our republics. . . . seem never to have recollected the danger from legislative usurpations; which by assembling all power in the same hands, must lead to the same tyranny as is threatened by executive usurpations.
>
> . . . in a representative republic, where the executive magistracy is carefully limited both in the extent and duration of its power; and where the legislative power is exercised by an assembly, which is inspired by a supposed influence over the people with an intrepid confidence in its own strength; which is sufficiently numerous to feel all passions which actuate a multitude; yet not so numerous as to be incapable of pursuing the objects of its passions, by means which reason prescribes; it is against the enterprising ambition of this department, that the people ought to indulge all their jealousy and exhaust all their precautions.[72]

Certainly with this conception of the legislative power it is understandable that no effort was made to remind Congress of its duties.[73] This conception is reflected in Madison's subsequent exposition of the system of checks and balances as a set of rules that is aimed partly at securing executive and judicial independence from Congress.[74]

Perhaps a more basic reason for not including a reminder respecting the duty to exercise congressional power lies in what may be the most significant decision of the founding generation, the decision to substitute checks and balances for a reliance on official and citizen virtue as the primary method for maintaining the constitutional order.[75] At one point Madison described the system of checks and balances as a "policy of supplying by opposite and rival interests, the defect of better motives. . . . that the private interest of every individual, may be a sentinel over public rights."[76] Such a scheme would not necessitate language wherein the notion of duty predominates. Nevertheless, Madison could not have spoken of the policy of supplying the defect of better motives had he not held a guiding image of better motives. "Ambition," he said "must be made to counteract ambition. The interest of the man must be connected with the rights of the place."[77] And for what other reason, we might ask, than that the rights of the place might be exercised as by one who felt a duty to exercise them?[78]

Never more than slightly submerged in the concept of instrumental powers, the notion of constitutional duty comes to the surface in such requirements as the presidential oath, the state of the union message, and the injunction to "take Care that the Laws be faithfully executed." It is visible also in the requirement that Congress meet at least once a year, that it keep a journal of its proceedings, and in the provision that the attendance of absent members may be compelled by minorities of each house.[79] Marshall saw it when he spoke of the "province and duty of the judicial department to say what the law is,"[80] and when he insisted that congressional power be so interpreted as to "enable that body to perform the high duties assigned to it, in the manner most beneficial to the people."[81] Lincoln saw it when he declared before Congress that loyal citizens "have the right" to demand the preservation of the government so "that it may be administered for all. . . . and the Government has no right to withhold or neglect it."[82] In our era Roosevelt inaugurated his administration with the pledge that he would perform his "constitutional duty to recommend the measures that a stricken nation . . . may require," adding that "in the event that the Congress shall fail to take these courses. . . . I shall not evade the clear course of duty that will then confront me."[83] While not always a feature of our constitutional consciousness, the notion of constitutional duty is thus present not only in our constitutional logic but also on the surface of the constitutional document and in the rhetoric of our political leadership.

By this reasoning, Congress does not necessarily have an obligation to perform every task that it is able to perform itself. Congress may delegate decisions to others, even important decisions, as long as these delegations appear to be necessary and proper exercises of power—in other words, as long as it can be said that Congress has arrived at a clear policy decision among salient alternatives and that the delegations in question are instrumental to such decisions. Just how specific such decisions must be is a matter of judgment that cannot be fully determined by formula. But these judgments should be structured by the rule that Congress has no constitutional basis for delegating power as a substitute for decision: Congress may delegate only as an instrument of decision. Accordingly, decision of some kind among substantive policy alternatives there must be, and whatever delegation takes place must be fairly adjudged instrumental to that decision.[84] Only then could a delegation be understood as an exercise of power.

Perhaps this conclusion brings us as far as a discussion of general principles might safely go. It may now be time to apply theoretical principles to concrete cases in order to see some of the practical effects of those principles. Before turning to the cases, however, it should be noted that the idea of constitutional duty elaborated here contributes a set of general guidelines for applying the rule to cases as well as some suggestions for the spirit in which that task should be conducted.

First, there is the matter of the kind of inquiry appropriate in delegation cases. If Congress may delegate pursuant to decisions among salient policy alternatives, it follows that the controlling considerations in delegation cases should involve the nature of congressional decision, not the character of the power delegated.[85] Instead of asking whether "discretionary" or "ministerial powers" have been delegated, how much discretion has resulted, or whether the functions transferred are fairly described as "legislative," let us ask whether Congress has authorized rule-making by others out of irresolution and in order to evade its responsibilities or as a means to exercising its power of choice among competing policies.

A related problem concerns the stage of statutory history to which the delegation doctrine should apply. If the controlling considera-tion in delegation cases should be the nature of congressional decision, not the nature of power exercised by those who administer congressional decisions, it would appear that the delegation question is appropriate to the decision made at the time of enactment only. Failure of Congress to recover control of administrative activity may be related to an original delegation, but since failure to recover is not identical to the act of delegation it is difficult to see how failure to recover could invalidate the original act. As stated before, problems resulting from delegations and, therefore, parts of what might be termed the "delegation problem," extend beyond the scope of the "rule of nondelegation" as interpreted here.

As an example of the manner in which these first two guidelines structure the delegation inquiry for a given case, let us consider the issue of the president's right to impound funds appropriated by statute. Is there a constitutional requirement that the president spend appropriated money? This issue proves to be a compound of several different issues, including the following. Is the act of impounding "legislative" or "executive" in nature? Does it constitute an item veto unauthorized by the Constitution? May Congress delegate the power to impound? Of these and other questions, the one that concerns us here is obviously the third. As we look at the third question, however, we can see how it might be possible for its answer to be influenced by suppositions relative to the other two questions. We might want to say that Congress may not delegate the power to impound either because that power is essentially legislative, or because the use of that power constitutes a prohibited item veto. From the narrow perspective of the delegation doctrine as analyzed here, however, the nature of the power delegated is irrelevant to the delegation question. The delegation, as a delegation, may be valid even though a legislative function is said to be involved. And this delegation, as such, may be valid even though the use of the power delegated may offend the Constitution on other grounds. The sole question in the present context is whether Congress delegates pursuant to a policy choice or in order to evade the responsibility for choice.

Hence, by limiting our inquiry to the delegation question we would at best be able to address only a small part of the "impounding issue." For even if we were to decide that a given congressional act of delegating the impounding power were invalid, the particular presidential act of impounding may still be held valid on other grounds. Impounding might still be adjudged an executive prerogative, for example.[86]

A further restriction on our inquiry arises from the stage of legislative history to which the delegation question is appropriate. The Budget Act of 1950 delegated broad impounding powers to the president. We shall comment further on this delegation below, but for the moment we can assume *arguendo* that the delegation is constitutional. However, to say that it is constitutional means only that Congress delegated pursuant to a policy choice at the time of delegation. It is not to say or predict that the act will not come to be counted as an instrument for the evasion of congressional duty under future circumstances. The authorization to impound may have expressed a policy choice in 1950, but at a later date that same statutory authorization may, in changed political circumstances, have the effect of insulating Congress from the duty to decide between different policy alternatives. Accordingly, one might correctly state at a later date that by not repealing the decision of 1950 Congress is permitting the president to nullify statutory intent with respect to spending priorities.[87] Hypothetically, the same statutory language might have been an expression of congressional irresolution if passed at a later date, for it might then have delegated power to nullify Congress' own professed priorities. Nevertheless, the act of 1950 may have been constitutional when it was passed. At a later date Congress may possibly be adjudged guilty of an evasion of responsibility by not repealing the decision of 1950. But the failure to repeal is not the same as the original act of delegation. Of course, one could argue that the same norms of congressional duty which would prohibit such a delegation at a later date would mandate repeal at that time. That may be, but the delegation question would still concern only the validity of the delegation, not the issue of repeal. Questions of congressional responsibility, duty, irresolution, abdication, and the like, are simply broader than problems of the legitimacy of congressional delegations. And the former cannot be resolved completely by the rule of nondelegation.

A third set of problems concerns legislative standards in the statutes delegating power. How specific should these standards be? Are they necessary in every case? If our interest in each case is the nature of the decision reached by Congress, it would appear that the essential requirement of statutory language is that it accurately communicate the decision made. Statutory standards should be required simply in order that the public might know what policies are being pursued. Ideally, it should not be necessary for the public to research the legislative history of an act to learn the major decisions made at the time of enactment. As for the specificity of standards, our analysis suggests that specificity is a quality which should be relative not to preexisting verbal criteria which cut across all cases but to the actual level of decision in each case. Sometimes the most salient issues facing Congress are expressed in terms exhibiting high specificity; at other times terms of low specificity characterize the debate. The most important thing is that the language of the statute correctly reflect the decision made and that the decision not express irresolution relative to the salient policy alternatives.

Nevertheless, sometimes standards may appear so nebulous on their face that one is compelled to question the validity of the delegation. Let us again consider the Budget Act of 1950, which states, in part:

> In apportioning any appropriation, reserves may be established to provide for contingencies, or to effect savings whenever savings are made possible by or through changes in requirements, greater efficiency of operations, or other developments subsequent to the date on which such appropriation was made available.[88]

Some have suggested that by this language power is delegated to the president to impound funds whenever he thinks he has a good reason to do so—even when his reasons can fairly be said to run counter to congressional policy in specific cases.[89] If such were the conscious intent of Congress at the time of delegation, the act would be an evasion of a constitutional duty and unconstitutional on that account. But in order to determine this, the standards of the statute would have to be measured against the issues held salient by Congress at the time of delegation. To expose these issues, an investigation of the legislative history of the delegation might be necessary. In an investigation of legislative history we would seek statements of the salient issues at the time of enactment in order to determine whether the statutory standards express a clear choice between the alternatives Congress faced.

In the conduct of such an investigation there might be no way to avoid difficult judgments at several junctures. To identify a rather large problem of judgment, the observer of congressional action may often have a number of choices in determining what issues were salient at the time of enactment, a central question in findings of congressional intent and the adequacy of statutory standards. This difficulty can be seen in the testimony of Joseph Cooper on the impounding issue before the Senate Subcommittee on Separation of Powers in March 1971.[90]

In a single piece of testimony, Cooper offers two different versions of the quality of congressional intent in the Budget Act of 1950. Confining himself to the more immediate facts in the legislative history of Section 665(c)(2), quoted in part above, Cooper states that it was "intended by Congress simply . . . to effect savings" in certain types of circumstances, not to authorize the executive "to frustrate the purposes of Congress." Cooper says that this was also the professed understanding of the Budget Bureau in presenting the bill.[91] If this is a fair description of congressional intent, the section hardly seems an expression of congressional irresolution.

Nevertheless, by enlarging somewhat the historical context to include the issues of the impounding debate in the years preceding the act, the language of Section 665(c)(2) may indeed express congressional irresolution. This is seen in other parts of Cooper's analysis.

Cooper points out that in 1950 Congress approached the latest of four stages of the impounding problem. The first stage had begun in the early 1920s, not by virtue of statutory authorization to impound, but by virtue of executive inferences from the Budget and Accounting Act of 1921 that in apportioning funds to prevent deficiencies it was also desirable to impound funds in order to effect whatever savings were consistent with the pursuit of the program goals set by statute. The second stage expanded this practice to the point of effecting savings by imposing a certain percentage cut on the budget overall. In 1931, for example, President Hoover imposed an overall budget cut of 10 percent, controlling in this way, says Cooper, "the tempo or rate of program implementation in an overall sense." By the mid-thirties a third stage was developing, as impoundments were used by the executive to control the rate of implementing specific programs. This power evolved in the early 1940s to that of "achievement or execution of particular programs per se." Cooper also notes that this power "led to a continuing and bitter battle with Congress throughout the whole course of the war with the President's actions coming under constant attack by the Congress." This use of the impounding power continued beyond the war.[92]

Such, according to Cooper, was the background of the Budget Act of 1950. The goal towards which the impounding power aimed in the early 1920s can be identified generally by the term "savings," but savings which were at least theoretically compatible with the pursuit of congressional policy. Such was not always the case by 1950. The power to effect savings compatible with legislative purposes had evolved into a power to effect savings even when not compatible with legislative purposes. A question of the act of 1950, from Cooper's perspective, was whether Congress was prepared to give explicit statutory authority for impoundments that could defeat legislative purposes. As Cooper sees it, the language of the Budget Act did not answer this question in a clear manner.[93]

Indeed, it might be said that Congress was unable to make a clear policy choice on the general use of impoundments. Cooper says that "even after Congress perceived that impoundment could indeed threaten its legislative will or purpose, its desire for economy blunted any counterattack either to put an end to impoundment or to confine the executive simply to impoundments that did not seriously threaten program objectives."[94] He argues that while the language of the Budget Act, adopted substantially as proposed by the executive branch, suggested that savings would not interfere with legislative purposes, the language was elastic, and Congress should have narrowed it further to make its intentions clear.[95] As it turned out, the language was construed narrowly for a time. But it was inherently broad enough to authorize "without a great deal of stretching" impoundments to govern the rate of program implementation and even the "achievement of a program per se."[96] As a result of conflicting congressional motives, Cooper concludes, the act of 1950, "despite its wording . . . did not restrict subsequent exercises of withholding or impoundment, but rather has served as a platform for sizable growth or expansion of the practice in the fifties and sixties."[97]

As the conflict in Cooper's testimony shows, this is a difficult delegation to evaluate. If the observer confines his analysis to the language of the act and to the initial presentations of the executive branch in behalf of the bill, the delegation was not an expression of congressional irresolution relative to the value of "savings" and the program goals for which funds were appropriated. The delegation would be constitutional on this hypothesis despite the fact that it was subsequently stretched by the executive to a power to defeat the statutory purposes of Congress. On the other hand, by enlarging one's perspective to include the history of the impounding power up to that time, one can legitimately question, as Cooper does, congressional resolve to confine impoundments to those not incompatible with statutory purposes.

In the face of this kind of difficulty, the statutory standards of Section 665 (c) (2) provide little help. For even though they might be reasonably specific in a verbal sense, they may still not enable differentiations among the policy alternatives which may have faced Congress at the time. An investigation into the legislative history of the act would improve the observer's chances for an unprejudiced description of the policy intended by Congress, although one might not escape reasonable doubts even then. In any event, an investigation of legislative history would appear necessary for an attempt to answer the delegation question presented by the act.

An approach to the delegation question which focuses analysis on the nature of congressional decision while subordinating consideration of such statutory characteristics as the verbal specificity of statutory standards and the degree of discretion transferred, may raise problems for jurists adverse to deciding constitutional questions on the basis of legislative histories. Dean Alfange[98] traces the reluctance of some judges to examine underlying legislative "motives" in the face of statutory clarity and propriety to Chief Justice Marshall's opinion in *Fletcher v. Peck*.[99] He reports that the issue of examining legislative intent reached its greatest significance in the period of dual federalism when Congress was using the commerce and taxing powers to regulate what were regarded as intrastate activities.[100] He also notes the presence of the issue in civil liberties cases, particularly those inquiring into proper legislative purposes behind classifications challenged on equal protection grounds.[101]

Those jurists who avoid examining underlying legislative motives in constitutional cases express several reasons, including a reluctance to impute unconstitutional motives to a coordinate branch of government,[102] an appreciation of the difficulty and frequently the impossibility of discerning motives shared by the legislative majority as a whole,[103] and what appears to be a simple respect for the form of an enactment valid on its face.[104] Limiting the idea of legislative "motives" to the general "purposes" or "policy" of an enactment, as opposed to the underlying individual reasons for supporting a policy, Alfange insists on the validity and necessity of examining legislative history.[105] "It would be an unfortunate doctrine," he says, "that a constitutionally forbidden purpose could be achieved without fear of judicial invalidation so long as it was accomplished by means of a statute that, on its face, was innocuous."[106] He finds that, in fact, "this is not a rule of constitutional law, for the United States Reports are rife with judicial declarations that legislatures cannot attain an invalid end in the guise of exercising a valid power."[107]

We need do no more here than note that the propriety of legislative histories is a matter of dispute among jurists. Our guidelines for applying the delegation doctrine derive from what we perceive to be necessary evidentiary processes for determining whether Congress has acted constitutionally. Thus, our guidelines are shaped by what are seen as the requirements of an effective constitutionalism and the need for frameworks and procedures of inquiry based on these requirements. Assuming that our understanding of constitutional requirements is correct, it is that understanding which defines our obligations. Whatever the ways of some judges, there seems little basis for denying the utility and validity of legislative histories in determining certain constitutional questions. A reluctance to impute unconstitutional motives to legislatures is hardly beyond challenge in view of the fact that constitutionalism makes little sense in the absence of the assumption that government can and will try to act unconstitutionally. Concerning a respect for the form of a valid enactment, such respect should not be carried to the point of ignoring the difference between form and substance. And neither law, political science, nor citizenship would be possible if we were typically unable to describe an enactment in terms of its general policy aims and the political conflicts and needs which give meaning to those aims.

However, this is not to pretend that we shall be able to make judgments free of problems in every case we might consider. Sometimes the evidence will simply not support a reasonably confident choice between conflicting descriptions of an act. If, for example, we were to look no further than Cooper's testimony for evidence on the impounding delegation in the Budget Act of 1950, we might not be able to decide whether it was an expression of congressional irresolution or not. In principle, evidence is possible for answering questions of congressional purposes relative to alternatives considered salient by Congress. But this does not mean that a satisfactory level of evidence will be available to observers in each case. Judges who face such problems may feel obligated to decide the case before them in any event. But neither the citizen nor the academic observer appear governed by norms compelling decision in the presence of evidence which seems inconclusive.

A fourth consideration in applying the delegation doctrine concerns the identity of the recipient of delegated power. Legislatures, of course, do not confine their delegations to administrative and executive agencies. The Supreme Court has held delegations to nongovernmental agencies as "delegation in its most obnoxious form" because private groups may not exercise delegated power in a "presumptively disinterested" way.[108] Congressional delegations to state agencies have been opposed,[109] as have those of state legislatures to their constituencies.[110] Deliberate congressional delegations to courts in the form of vague statutory standards have also been criticized as evasions of responsibility.[111] Because the delegation doctrine is properly grounded in the concepts of constitutional supremacy and constitutional duty, and not in concepts like separated powers, due process, and representative government, the question of who receives delegated power is irrelevant here. We are not concerned with the fitness of the recipient to exercise power. We are concerned with the character of congressional decision. From the narrow perspective of the delegation doctrine, Congress may delegate to any agency, public or private, administrative, judicial, or whatever, as long as its delegations are pursuant to choice among salient alternatives. Congress violates the rule of nondelegation when it deliberately evades its responsibility for choice no matter how it may delegate or to whom.

Finally, before turning to cases we should ask for the spirit of applying the rule suggested by our analysis. We have reformulated the rule of nondelegation in terms of such concepts as the duty of Congress to exercise its power and the duty to avoid delegation from irresolution. We have also extracted from our analysis several general guidelines concerning the nature, the locus, and the scope of the delegation question. These reformulations and guidelines may have meaning in debate on general principles, but in applying them to concrete cases we can expect to discover that sometimes our categories subsume not one but several alternatives. By what values might we be guided in questions that elude solution by formula?

The rule of nondelegation as analyzed here manifests a particular balance of several values: most generally, the values of constitutional authority and stability and the values of governmental responsiveness to the interests and inclinations of its constituents. In every balance of potentially conflicting values, however, one set predominates, and in this case the prevailing set is constitutional stability and authority—even at the expense of responsive government if and when a choice between the two is necessary. But this is nothing new. Nondelegation has strong historical connections with concepts associated with a legalistic, restrictive view of constitutional government.

On the other hand, while one set of values predominates in every balance, each set is compromised, and the set compromised most in this case is the restrictive legalism at the basis of the delegation doctrine. This is indicated by our attempt to find for the delegation doctrine the firmest constitutional ground and the discovery that in doing so we have narrowed the doctrine to all but its least restrictive scope. Nondelegation grounded in constitutional supremacy is simply not as restrictive as nondelegation grounded in separation of powers, due process of law, and legislative supremacy. Nor is the delegation doctrine necessarily in conflict with the philosophy of the positive state. On the contrary, because it seeks to prohibit the evasion of certain duties and responsibilities, the rule of nondelegation is at least as positive as any other norm of the Constitution, expressed or implied. The rule of nondelegation, construed in accordance with its proper logical foundation, belongs to a family of norms at the basis of constitutional arguments for the positive state: the supremacy clause, the necessary and proper clause, and the agency theory of the Preamble. With these norms the rule of nondelegation can be construed as pointing simultaneously to the social needs government ought to serve and to a basic arrangement of offices and powers through which those ends should be pursued.

With this balance of values in mind, we may justify the approval of any delegation of power which fairly represents an effort by Congress to exercise its responsibility for decision among what it regards as the salient alternatives facing it. Accordingly, we are free to apply the delegation doctrine in a permissive spirit until we are satisfied that Congress is deliberately evading the responsibility of decision and choice.

As an example of the kind of delegations which might be approved under the present conception, let us consider the delegation of power not as an instrument of congressional policy already determined but as a technique for developing material for decisions yet to be made. Suppose Congress delegates from indecision in the face of major alternatives, not with the intent of evading decision, but with hopes that through a period of administrative experience with a problem a more reliable basis for decision will emerge. Such a delegation might be described both as a delegation from irresolution and as a delegation through which Congress seeks to exercise its responsibilities for decision. The balance of values behind our conception of the rule suggests that such delegations might be approved if Congress were to commit itself to a future declaration of policy. Such delegations might be saved through provisions for mandatory review within a specified period of statutory duration. As long as provisions for review and reenactment did not themselves become techniques for perpetuating and legitimizing evasions, they could enable delegations from irresolution to be classified as instruments of decision. Congress, to modify Davis's oft-quoted passage would thus be saying: "Here is the problem. Show *us* how *we* might deal with it."[112]

Delegation cases in
Supreme Court history

The principles of analysis developed in the preceding part of our discussion now can be applied to some of the Supreme Court's leading delegation cases. The review of cases that follows will focus both on problems of describing congressional action in a manner relevant to the delegation doctrine and on versions of the doctrine formulated by the Court. The activity of applying these standards will enable us to understand further their practical and theoretical implications.

The cases included in this review have been selected as representative of the major phases of the delegation doctrine's judicial development. The first group of cases concerns congressional power to delegate the power to determine facts on which statutory results shall be contingent. The second group of cases concerns the power of Congress to delegate the filling-up of legislative details as distinguished from responsibility for important subjects of legislation reserved for regulation by Congress itself. The concepts and patterns of decision in these early phases of the rule produced the modern theory that delegations are constitutional as long as they are accompanied by clear statutory statements of congressional policy for the guidance of administrators and reviewing courts. The third and final section of the review will consider cases that both represent and deviate from the modern doctrine. While the cases selected for evaluation are grouped in historical order, there are departures from historical order within each group, as required by analytic considerations. The principal aim here, as elsewhere in this study, is to elaborate what are regarded as proper principles, not to trace the evolution of historical doctrine.

Perhaps it is unnecessary to add that in law and in science the indexing and application of general concepts involve judgments which are going to be controversial in some measure, on some level. In the effort facing us there may be no way to apply the standards of our analysis in a manner that will earn universal agreement. Other observers will undoubtedly apply the same standards with different results. But the apparent inevitability of disagreement in evaluations of particular actions and events is a poor basis for abandoning altogether the effort to formulate and apply standards. We may disagree, for example, over the proper elaboration of the concept of congressional responsibility. We may also disagree as to how a specific elaboration of that concept should be applied to a particular action or event. However, the search for the best understanding of congressional responsibility is conducted largely through such disagreement. And precisely because it would be a good thing to have and to live under the best understanding, the search for it is also a good thing.

Delegations of Fact-finding Power
The Brig Aurora v. United States and Field v. Clark

The earliest and logically the most restrictive form of delegation permitted by the federal courts was the power to declare the facts on which the operation or suspension of congressional policy was contingent. The two most important cases in this area are *The Brig Aurora* v. *United States* (1813),[1] and *Field* v. *Clark* (1892).[2] The concepts and patterns of judicial decision developed or expressed in these cases have had significant effects on the subsequent evolution of the delegation doctrine.

The Brig Aurora v. United States

This case arose from difficulties in foreign affairs suffered by the United States in its efforts to remain neutral during the Napoleonic

Wars. In 1806–7 England and France each issued decrees blockading the other's ports and obstructing the shipping of neutral nations with the other. American interests were adversely affected by these decrees, and the American government took several steps to protect those interests. Among these was the Non-Intercourse Act of March 1809, an act aimed at stopping trade with England and France in retaliation for their seizures and other harassments of American shipping. The Aurora case was an appeal from the sentence of a district court condemning the cargo of the brig Aurora for having been imported from Great Britain in violation of the Non-Intercourse Act of March 1809, as revived by an act of May 1810, and a presidential proclamation provided for by the latter act.

One of the questions of the case turned on the issue of whether the presidential proclamation had been issued under the authority of an unconstitutional delegation of congressional power. Section 4 of the act of May 1810, enacted

> that in case either Britain or France shall, before the third day of March next, so revoke or modify her edicts, as they shall cease to violate the neutral commerce of the United States, which fact the President of the United States shall declare by proclamation, and if the other nation shall not within three months thereafter so revoke or modify her edicts in like manner, then [sections of the Non-Intercourse Act of March 1809] ... shall be revived ... as relates to the dominions, colonies, and dependencies of the nation thus refusing or neglecting to revoke or modify her edicts in manner aforesaid. And the restrictions imposed by this act shall, from the date of such proclamation, cease and be discontinued in relation to the nation revoking or modifying her decrees in manner aforesaid.[3]

Counsel for the appellant claimed that this language constituted a transfer of legislative power to the president. "To make the revival of a law depend upon the President's proclamation, is to give to that proclamation the force of law," he argued.[4] The government responded simply that "The legislature did not transfer any power of legislation to the President. They only prescribed the evidence which should be admitted of a fact, upon which the law should go into effect."[5] And the Court, through Justice Johnson, held with the government that

> we can see no sufficient reason why the legislature should not

exercise its discretion in reviving the act of March first 1809 either expressly or conditionally as their judgment should direct.[6]

Thus, the most relevant consideration for the Court was not the quality of the president's judgment, but the legislative judgment which made the president's proclamation a mere contingency for the actualization of a legislative decision.

In view of the paucity of discussion on the point by all sides not much should be made of the fact that the Court failed to respond directly to the charge that legislative power had been tranferred to the president. Indeed, the Court may have been forced into this approach by an act of March 2, 1811, in which Congress sought to forbid judicial review of the factual finding behind the president's proclamation.[7] Nevertheless, the approach employed by the Court is noteworthy as an example of what we have presented in the preceding chapter as the preferred approach. The appellant had charged that Section 4 constituted a transfer of legislative power. The government responded with the contrary position that Section 4 did not transfer power of legislation to the president. For whatever reason, the Court ignored questions concerning the nature of the power being exercised by the president and shifted instead to a focus on congressional intent. From the perspective of Congress at the time of enactment, the presidential proclamation was to be based on a mere factual contingency—irrespective of whatever legislative qualities the president's judgment might have exhibited *later* to the president himself, to such third parties as the Court and the appellant, and even to a later Congress.[8]

This case is widely cited as the basis for the constitutionality of a type of delegation known as "contingent legislation." "Here," as Pritchett explains it, "the delegation is not of power to make rules or fill in details; it is delegation of authority to determine facts or make predictions which are to have the effect of suspending legislation, or alternatively, of bringing it into effect."[9] As later expanded in the Court's review of the flexible tariff arrangements of the McKinley tariff in *Field* v. *Clark,* the authority to determine facts is understood as distinguishable from the authority to exercise discretion among conflicting policy alternatives.[10] At first glance the distinction between factual determinations and policy judgments at the root of the concept of contingent legislation is easier to criticize in *Field* v. *Clark* than it is in *The Brig Aurora.* In the former case the "facts" to be ascertained concerned the imposition by foreign nations on certain American goods of tariffs deemed to be "reciprocally unequal and unreasonable." Commenting on the factual qualities of a presidential finding that certain duties are "reciprocally unequal and unreasonable," Jaffe remarks that

> This apparently simple arithmetic for action concealed a wide and uncertain area of judgment. The alleged equivalence between some rate on, let us say, a ton of steel exported by us to Cuba and the free entry of a ton of sugar from Cuba is sheer illusion. It is not a formula at all but a bargaining power put into the President's hands in his conduct of foreign affairs.[11]

Presumably much less discretion was placed in the president's hands by the act of May 1810, which called for a simple factual declaration of whether certain formal edicts had been revoked by a specified date. Of the act of May 1810, Jaffe says that "The adminstrative element in the act was comparatively slight, though the determination whether France or England had ceased 'to violate neutral commerce' did require the exercise of some judgment."[12]

Indeed it did. The act of May 1810, known as Macon's Bill No. 2, was passed following the collapse of the nonintercourse policies against England and France. The bill was designed to restore trade with the two belligerents even in the presence of their continuing violations of America's neutrality. But at the same time, the bill presented the selective reimposition of nonintercourse as an inducement for revoking decrees inimical to American shipping. Its initial effect, in view of the relative strength of British and French naval power, was to benefit England. Napoleon treated it, in Channing's words, as "hardly less than entering into alliance with Great Britain."[13] However, Channing adds, Napoleon also found in the act "a clear road for the hoodwinking of the United States, and perhaps, forcing her into war with Great Britain."[14] Napoleon's strategy included the announcement that his decrees were revoked but that they would not cease to have effect until some four months after the decree of revocation, during which time the English should revoke their orders or the United States should compel the English to respect its rights.

Obviously, Napoleon's strategy raised the question whether the French decrees were in fact revoked or were to be revoked on some further contingency under the control of the British and American governments.[15] Madison relied upon the formal aspect of the French move, issued the proclamation of November 2, 1810 (one day after the French deadline) declaring that the edicts had been "revoked" and, in conformity with Macon's Bill No. 2, gave England three months to modify her edicts or suffer the revival of the Non-Intercourse Act.

For over a year and a half, until driven by internal economic distress in June 1812, Great Britain refused to revoke her edicts on the simple grounds that France had not in fact rescinded her antineutral edicts. Morison writes that "almost every mail, for the next two years [after Madison's proclamation] brought news of fresh seizures and scuttlings of American vessels by French port authorities, warships, and privateers. But Madison, having taken his stand, obstinately insisted that 'the national faith was pledged to France.' "[16] Henry Adams charged that Madison "by proclaiming the French Decrees to be revoked ... made himself a party to Napoleon's fraud."[17] On Madison's "factual" proposition that Napoleon had revoked the decrees of Milan and Berlin, Adams commented with exasperation that

> The United States had the right to make war on England with or without notice, either for her past spoliations, her actual blockades, her Orders in Council other than blockades, her Rule of 1756, her impressments, or for her attack on the "Chesapeake," not yet redressed,—possibly also for others less notorious; but the right to make war did not carry with it the right to require that the world should declare to be true an assertion which the world knew to be false. Unless England were a shrew to be tamed, President Madison could hardly insist on her admitting the sun to be the moon; and so well was Congress aware of this difficulty that it waited in silence for two months, until, February 2, the President's proclamation went into effect; while the longer Congress waited, the greater became its doubts.[18]

Ironically, Congress chose to settle doubts concerning the delegation to the president through statutory revival of nonintercourse against Great Britain in the act of March 2, an act which prohibited the courts from reviewing the question of whether the French edicts were actually revoked.[19]

Returning to the arguments in *The Brig Aurora,* we can see immediately the weakness in the government's response that "the legislature did not transfer any power of legislation to the President." President Madison's controversial proclamation pursuant to Macon's Bill No. 2 was considerably more than a simple factual judgment concerning the revocation of Napoleon's edicts. In declaring the edicts revoked, Madison chose to interpret the facts in accordance with Napoleon's design and contrary to the perceptions of the British, of prominent congressional leaders in and out of the Republican party, and even contrary to his personal interpretation as expressed privately to Jefferson.[20] As an act among conflicting interpretations, each with real and largely predictable consequences for the immediate future and each with its own set of partisans, Madison's proclamation was substantially more than a mechanical administration of congressional will. The proclamation was a policy choice, not a factual judgment in accordance with congressional preconditions. In terms of the power Madison ended up exercising as a result of the congressional delegation, the government was wrong in contending that "the legislature did not transfer any power of legislation to the President," and Madison persuaded no one with the fiction that the decision involved no discretion on his part. The appellant was correct in arguing that, in this case, "To make the revival of a law depend on the President's proclamation, is to give that proclamation the force of law."

The virtue of the Court's opinion is that it upheld the delegation without the myth-making characteristic of later delegation decisions. Justice Johnson managed to avoid saying that the president was exercising a mere fact-finding function. He did this by declining to handle the question as framed by the litigants. The question Johnson answered was whether Congress could revive the Non-Intercourse Act on the basis of a contingency to be declared by the president. Johnson was noncommittal on the question of presidential discretion in arriving at the declaration.

The Court had little trouble with the case because it looked at the question from the point of view of Congress prior to the complications brought about by Napoleon's strategy. In Macon's Bill No. 2 Congress made a clear decision to restore trade with Great Britain and France, with the provisions of Section 4 added as inducements to each of the belligerents to exempt the United States from its edicts. Although there was some recognition in Congress that presidential discretion would be involved to a degree,[21] the matter received little comment, and the decision to delegate was pursuant to a clear policy choice. Given congressional expectations at the time the delegation was made, Napoleon, not Congress, forced Madison into the weighty decision he was to make. Whether Madison was authorized to make the decision into which Napoleon forced him, and whether the decision made was or even should have been in conformity with congressional intentions, are questions beyond the scope of the delegation doctrine. However they might be answered, the delegation itself was constitutional.

Field v. Clark

Nearly eighty years later, in *Field v. Clark,* the Court relied on *The Brig Aurora* to uphold the delegation in Section 3 of the Tariff Act of 1890. But Justice Harlan's approach to the delegation problem in the act of 1890 was significantly different from Justice Johnson's in Macon's Bill No. 2. In attempting what Johnson had avoided, a denial of the discretionary character of an act of presidential "fact-finding," Harlan contributed to trapping the nondelegation doctrine in the untenable verbalisms which have provoked the ridicule of later commentary. The delegation itself was constitutional but certainly not because Congress had transferred a nondiscretionary fact-finding task.

Section 3 of the act read in part as follows:

That with a view to secure reciprocal trade with countries producing the following articles . . . whenever and so often as the President shall be satisfied that the government of any country producing and exporting sugars, molasses [and other named aritcles] imposes duties or other exactions upon the agricultural or other products of the United States, which in view of the free introduction of such sugar, molasses [and other named articles] into the United States, he may deem to be reciprocally unequal and unreasonable, he shall have the power and it shall be his duty to suspend, by proclamation to that effect, the provisions of this Act relating to the free introduction of such sugar, molasses [and other named articles] for such time as he shall deem just.[22]

In upholding the provision, Justice Harlan stated:

The Act. . . does not, in any real sense, invest the President with the power of legislation. . . . He had no discretion in the premises except in respect to the duration of the suspension so ordered. But that related only to the enforcement of the policy established by Congress. As the suspension was absolutely required when the

President ascertained the existence of a particular fact, it cannot be said that in ascertaining that fact and in issuing his proclamation, in obedience to the legislative will, he exercised the function of making laws. Legislative power was exercised when Congress declared that the suspension should take effect upon a named contingency.[23]

The fallacy in contending that Congress had delegated "no discretion in the premises except in respect to the duration of the suspension so ordered" is clear for at least two reasons. First, there is no commensurability between rates on different items. Jaffe, as noted above, terms "sheer illusion" the alleged arithmetic equivalence between rates on, say, a ton of exported steel and a ton of imported sugar. The concept of "reciprocally unequal" duties, Jaffe adds, "is not a formula at all, but a bargaining power put into the President's hands in his conduct of foreign affairs."[24] Second, even if there were some way to eliminate discretion in the decision concerning the reciprocal equality of rates, the president would still possess wide latitude for judgment in deciding whether foreign duties on American products were "unreasonable."

We can guess that the reasons for Justice Harlan's unrealistic approach included a desire to uphold the statute, a desire to support the doctrine of nondelegation,[25] and an understanding of the scope of the doctrine which necessitates a fictional rendition of the statute in order to save both. As Duff and Whiteside report the principal developments in the states up to that point, it appears that Justice Harlan was conforming to what had become a standard judicial practice in delegation cases.

In the early Delaware case of *Rice* v. *Foster* (1847),[26] cited above in connection with the implications for nondelegation in the idea of republican government, a local-option statute was attacked on delegation grounds. The defendant, citing *The Aurora,* defended the statute as follows:

It does not delegate legislative power. Legislative power is the power of making laws; not merely voting for or against laws made by others, but of proposing and maturing laws. The legislature passed this law. They expressed the judgment that such a law was beneficial to the community; and they declared the legislative will that such a law should exist, *if* a certain number, to wit, a majority of people of either county, should vote in a certain way.[27]

This argument contains two related steps which were to appear in later decisions upholding delegations. First, there was a division of the legislative function into different classes of actions, and, second, the challenged action was subsumed under that class to which the delegation doctrine did not apply. In *Rice* v. *Foster* the Delaware court rejected this approach to the problem of describing the legislature's action, reaffirmed a broad scope for the rule of nondelegation, and invalidated the statute.[28] The Pennsylvania Supreme Court, in *Parker* v. *Commonwealth* (1847), decided against a local option statute on grounds similar to *Rice* v. *Foster*.[29] However, the strict approach of these cases was steadily weakened in a number of cases authorizing voter decisions (in railway subscription and municipal annexations, for example), until *Parker* v. *Commonwealth* was overruled in *Locke's Appeal* (1873).[30] *Locke's Appeal*, cited by Harlan in *Field* v. *Clark*, upheld a local-option statute on the ground that the result of the local vote was a mere statutory contingency. The technique had appeared regularly in other states since the 1840s.[31]

It is important to note that in upholding these delegations the state courts made no appreciable retreat from the principle of nondelegation. On the contrary, strong affirmations of the principle remained a prominent feature of the opinions despite the principle's apparent erosion in the holdings. This disjunction between doctrine and holdings has understandably precipitated the widely held view that the contingency principle was used by the courts as a means of upholding the verbal aspects of the rule of nondelegation while escaping its practical consequences.[32] Such was the pattern of interpretation when *Field* v. *Clark* was decided, and Justice Harlan's opinion fit right into it. The opinion began with a strong affirmation of the rule of nondelegation as "vital to the integrity and maintenance of the system of government ordained by the Constitution" and ended with the fiction that the flexible-tariff provision left the president "no discretion in the premises except in respect to the duration of the suspension so ordered."[33]

On the basis of the theoretical reconstruction of the doctrine of nondelegation presented in this book, the approach of *Field* v. *Clark* is both unnecessary and counterproductive. Its central weakness is not the fictionalization of the discretionary act it is considering, but the implicitly expansive understanding of the rule of nondelegation it is applying. The courts which used this approach forced themselves into the alternatives of overruling reasonable delegations of legislative discretion or of unrealistically denying the fact that discretion had indeed been delegated—and all because they conceptualized the rule of nondelegation as proscribing all transfers of discretionary authority. This approach forced the courts into fruitless debates on whether a given legislative act was a "complete, positive, and absolute law in itself," or whether the function delegated was truly "legislative" in nature, or on what precisely was going to be regarded as a "completed" act of the "legislative" function.

This approach was counterproductive because it overlooked the fact that delegation of discretionary authority may be a necessary means to the exercise of power. Because the courts failed to reconcile the rule of nondelegation with the necessary and proper clause, the rule became too heavily encrusted with the constructs of judicial myth-making. Finally, the approach of *Field* v. *Clark* was unnecessary. If the courts wanted to sustain reasonable delegations, but desired at the same time to retain the rule of nondelegation as a device against unreasonable delegations, a more restricted understanding of the scope of the rule was needed.

Looking to the issues of the Tariff Act, we find some slight grounds for suspecting that the flexible-tariff provision was a technique for evading a choice between conflicting alternatives. In some respects the provision was tied to an effort to compensate for the effects on domestic consumers of an act which Taussig evaluated on the whole as a "radical extension of the protective system."[34] But given the circumstances leading to its proposal and the expectations of the manner in which it would be employed, the provision should be adjudged a measure pusuant to congressional policy.

The flexible-tariff provision, it will be noted, was tied to the abolition of duties on certain foreign products. The provision gave the president power to reimpose duties on goods from which duties had been lifted by Congress. Giving the president power to reimpose duties makes sense from a protectionist point of view—but why had a strongly protectionist Congress decided to admit these goods free in the first place? Taussig reported that duties on the goods covered by the flexible-tariff provision were abolished "as a means of gaining popularity for the new tariff act in the West, where the higher duties on manufactured articles might be difficult to present in an attractive light."[35] This might suggest that the flexible-tariff provision represented a bit of indecision on the part of an otherwise protectionist Congress, but it did not.

If, as Taussig concluded, the flexible-tariff provision was an effort to meet reaction in some quarters to the protectionist features of the bill, to the degree that the provision expressed values contrary to the bill's main thrust, it was a decision made by Congress itself. The discretion delegated to the president could move initially only in the direction of the bill's main thrust, without ever returning to a figure less than that which Congress had authorized in the first place. But even this much would have been true only of a few of the items since most of the duties previously imposed (on coffee, tea, and grades of raw sugar) were revenue duties primarily.[36] Therefore, in light of the nature of the discretion delegated to the president as well as the nature of most of the items covered, the flexible tariff was not an expression of congressional indecision. And while there was some doubt in Congress as to its justice, wisdom, and constitutionality, all were agreed that it was leverage to be exercised by the president in behalf of the domestic consumer.[37]

The Power of Filling Up Details: *Wayman* v. *Southard*

In addition to the idea of contingent legislation expressed in *The Brig Aurora* and in *Field* v. *Clark,* the second major tactic for approaching the delegation question in the early cases was the notion of delegation for purposes of "filling up the details" of general policies laid down by the legislature. The first Supreme Court decision employing this rationale was *Wayman* v. *Southard* (1825),[38] a case of considerable interest and importance because of the complexity of its facts and the provative qualities for delegation theory of the opinion of Chief Justice Marshall. The case is frequently cited as Marshall's contribution to our subject, but its theoretical potential has gone unappreciated—in part, no doubt, because of Marshall's own skill at insinuating seminal doctrine. Marshall's dicta in this area probably did not guide subsequent developments as they did in litigation under the commerce clause and the necessary and proper clause. Had they done so, however, it is doubtful that we could have had a more expansive doctrine. For hidden in Marshall's opinion there may be a theory of delegation as permissive as any ever held by a federal judge.

The second section of the Federal Process Act of 1792 read in part:

> That the form of writs, executions, and other process, except their style and the forms and modes of proceeding in suits, in those of Common Law, shall be the same as are now used in the said [state] courts ... except so far as may have been provided for by ... [the Judiciary Act of 1789] ... subject, however, to such alterations as the said [federal] courts respectively shall, in their discretion, deem expedient.[39]

Under this authorization federal judges in Kentucky adopted rules governing the manner of enforcing judgments and writs of execution which defeated, in suits brought in federal courts, state policy on procedure for the recovery of debts. In 1820 Kentucky incorporated the Bank of the Commonwealth of Kentucky and so controlled its capital and profits that it was "obviously nothing more than an arm of the state," according to Swisher.[40] By structuring its rules of judicial process—rules intended to apply to federal as well as state courts—the state sought to make notes of the bank acceptable in payment of debts. Rejecting the state's contention that its rules of process were binding on federal courts in Kentucky, the federal district court announced that its judgments could be satisfied only in gold and silver. In *Wayman* v. *Southard* Marshall upheld the position of the lower court.

Marshall's decsion contributed to a major constitutional uproar in Kentucky. Publicist and politician alike condemned what was widely regarded as a usurpation of the state's legislative power.[41] The sense of outrage was strong enough to find the Kentucky House of Representatives calling on the governor to inform it

> of the mode deemed most advisable, in the opinion of the Executive, to refuse obedience to the decisions and mandates of the Supreme Court of the United States considered erroneous and unconstitutional, and whether, in the opinion of the Executive, it may be advisable to call forth the physical power of the state to resist the execution of the decisions of the court, or in what manner the mandates of the said court should be met by disobedience.[42]

Congress enacted a new process law in May, 1828, making existing state process binding on the federal courts, but, again, granting to those courts the power to alter state process in the future. Kentucky congressmen continued to oppose such delegations of power, and the issue receded only as the passage of time brought changes in public opinion respecting the wisdom and necessity of statutes aimed at debtor relief.[43]

In upholding the delegation, Marshall reasoned, in part, as follows:

> It will not be contended that Congress can delegate to the courts, or to any other tribunals, powers which are strictly and exclusively legislative. But Congress may certainly delegate to others, powers which the legislature may rightfully exercise itself. . . .
>
> The line has not been exactly drawn which separates those important subjects, which must be entirely regulated by the legislature itself, from those of less interest, in which a general provision may be made, and power given to those who are to act under such general provisions to fill up the details. . . . The power given to the court to vary the mode of proceeding [in question] . . . is a power to vary minor regulations, which are within the great outlines marked out by the legislature in directing the execution. . . . It is, in all its parts, the regulation of the conduct of the officer of the court in giving effect to its judgments. . . . It is, undoubtedly, proper for the legislature to prescribe the manner in which these ministerial offices shall be performed, and this duty will never be devolved on any other department without urgent reasons. But, in the mode of obeying the mandate of a writ issuing from a court, so much of that which may be done by the judiciary, under the authority of the legislature, seems to be blended with that for which the legislature must expressly and directly provide, that there is some difficulty in discerning the exact limits within which the legislature may avail itself of the agency of its courts.
>
> The difference between the departments undoubtedly is, that the legislature makes, the executive executes, and the judiciary construes the law; but the maker of the law may commit something to the discretion of the other departments, and the precise boundary of this power is a subject of delicate and difficult inquiry into which a court will not enter unnecessarily.[44]

This statement features Marshallean ambiguity at each of the important junctures. On the one hand, there is a distinction between the power exclusively legislative and power conferred on the legislature which is not exclusively legislative. But when we come to inquire how this exclusively legislative power might be distinguished we are told that the line has not been exactly drawn which separates subjects deserving of legislative attention from those which can be entrusted to the hands of the legislature's agents. Moreover, that which is done under the authority of the legislature may be blended with that which the legislature must expressly and directly provide. A closer look at the opinion will show that it is a mistake to confine it to the interpretation that agents of the legislature may not engage in rule-making of great importance.[45]

It is true that Marshall says that agents of the legislature will be confined to subjects of "less interest." He also states that the legislature will deal with "important subjects." But he does not say in this case that the subjects of "less interest" are unimportant. When he uses the image of "filling up the details" he does not say that delegations will be restricted to matters of *mere* detail—nor could he have done so in view of what was at issue in this case.

The rules of process at issue in this case could be regarded as relatively less important that other basic decisions of policy which Congress might have made concerning the federal judiciary, but the political significance of the district court's decisions should not be underrated simply because there were more basic decisions to be made. The scope of the district court's decision is indicated in the following remarks of Kentucky's Senator Rowan in floor debate on the Process Act of 1828:

> Sir, you have in the rules of court, which have just been read, a full and complex code of execution laws including replevin— imprisonment for debt, and a system of conveyancing. The very highest exercises of sovereignty are exercised in conclave by these judges. They make their rules, which subject your property to seizure and sale, and your body to imprisonment.[46]

Rowan went on to commend a federal judge in Illinois who had refused to make process rules for his court. To Webster's contention that the Illinois judge was nevertheless free to do so, had he chosen to, Rowan exclaimed, "What! A District Judge of Illinois, possessing as much legislative power as can be exercised by the two Houses of Congress, and the President of the United States, united!"[47]

Despite rhetoric about filling up details and supplying minor regulations on less important subjects, Marshall was not unaware of the great political scope and significance of the "rules of court" at issue in the case. After remarking that "the maker of the law may commit something to the discretion of the other departments," and that "the precise boundary of this power is a subject of delicate and difficult inquiry, into which a court will not enter unnecessarily," Marshall followed with dicta which suggest a theory of delegation as permissive as any which has ever come from the Court. What was the policy of Congress to which the process rules stood related as "details"? Marshall gives the following explanation:

> Congress, at the introduction of the present government, was placed in a peculiar situation. A judicial system was to be prepared, not for a consolidated people, but for distinct societies already possessing distinct systems, and accustomed to laws, which, though originating in the same great principles, had been variously modified. The perplexity arising from this state of things was much augmented by the circumstance that, in many of the states, the pressure of the moment had produced deviations from that course of administering justice between debtor and creditor, which consisted, not only with the spirit of the Constitution, and, consequently, with the views of the government, but also with what might safely be considered as the permanent policy, as well as interest, of the states themselves. The new government could neither entirely disregard these circumstances, nor consider them as permanent. In adopting the temporary mode of proceeding with executions then prevailing in the several states, it was proper to provide for that return to ancient usage, and just as well as wise principles, which might be expected from those who had yielded to a supposed necessity in departing from them. Congress, probably, conceived that this object would be best effected by placing in the courts of the Union the power of altering the "modes of proceeding in suits at common law," which includes the modes of proceeding in the execution of their judgments, in the confidence, that in the exercise of this power, the ancient, permanent and approved system would be adopted by the courts, at least as soon as it should be restored in the several states by their respective legislatures. Congress could not have intended to give permanence to temporary laws of which it disapproved; and therefore, provided for their change in the very act which adopted them.[48]

Thus Marshall might have responded to Senator Rowan's attack on the establishment of process rules by the judiciary as the "very highest exercise of sovereignty" which subjects "your property to seizure and sale, and your body to imprisonment." Marshall's statement is remarkable because it indicates a conception of permissibility in delegations which is very broad indeed. The "details" which could be "filled up" by agents of Congress could be subsumed under objects as general as "that course of administering justice . . . which consisted . . . with the spirit of the Constitution, and . . . with what might safely be considered as the permanent policy, as well as interest, of the states themselves." Perhaps some modern legislative standards could be more broadly construed—after all, Marshall does not mention the "public convenience" in this formulation of the "public interest or necessity"—but surely not by much.

Another equally remarkable feature of Marshall's statement is the act of finding legislative intent in purposes beyond anything expressed in the statute and proclaiming those purposes to be the boundaries for administrative discretion authorized by the statute. Had Congress intended the objects for which, according to Marshall, "it was proper to provide"? Senator Rowan was to reply that Congress had something much less sweeping in mind:

> But, Sir, when did this idea of judicial legislation first present itself to the American People? The law of Congress authorizing the Judges to alter the forms of process, and to make rules, for the regulation of its own judicial proceeding in court, was, we all know, passed in 1789, and re-enacted in May, 1792. But nobody ever thought that either of these laws conferred legislative power upon the Judges. They themselves were unconscious of possessing any such power. The alternation of State process, in the article of form only, so as to adopt its use to the organic structure of the Federal Courts, was known to be all that was intended by Congress, in those acts. Nor, sir, did the Courts ever dream of exercising any other or further power under color of those acts, until since the war, and the establishment of the United States Bank. The experiment was first made in Kentucky, in the case, and under the auspices of that Bank—backed by all the talents, influence, and weight of character, which that institution possesses so amply the means of executing. The experiment was, unhappily, but too successful. The gentleman from Massachusetts [Webster] tells us that the invalidity of the Kentucky execution laws was a great evil, and that the Judges were called upon to apply the remedy. It is admitted to be the duty of the Judges to apply the remedy. But, it is asserted to be the right of the legislature to make it.[49]

Other suggestions of the senator aside, his understanding of congressional intent in the Process Act 1792 seems to have more support in the record than Marshall's. In fact, the one significant point of controversy in the debate resulted in the deliberate defeat of an amendment which would have broadened the power of the courts to defeat the rules of process established by the states. On February 13, 1792, the Senate, by a margin of one vote, contrary to the majority of the committee which had reported the process bill, voted to amend the bill so as to give creditors the "liberty to pursue" judgments in federal courts "until a tender of the debt and cost in gold or silver shall be made."[50] This amendment was rejected by the House on April 27. House opponents of the Senate amendment argued, in part, that it would "annihilate the power of the several states to pass insolvent laws; and in consequence, those unfortunate debtors would be entirely in the power of a set of persons who retained the most raucous enmity against the Revolution," and that it would vest "a power in a merciless creditor to immure an unfortunate debtor within the walls of a prison for life."[51] House supporters of the Senate amendment argued, in part, that the fear of merciless creditors was unsupported by experience, that "Uniformity, in connection with justice, was a principal object contemplated by the Constitution," and that to leave foreign creditors to the "Legislative provisions of the several States, which are known to clash, some of which have made paper a tender, others of which have depreciated paper in circulation, is to defeat every just expectation founded on the Treaty of Peace and the Constitution."[52]

Had the Senate's amendment prevailed, Marshall might have had fair evidence for his reconstruction of congressional intent. But House and Senate conferees were unable to agree on the Senate amendment,[53] and on May 7 the House reaffirmed its position of April 27.[54] On the evening of May 7, again by a close vote, the Senate agreed to accept the position of the House, and the amendment died.[55] This record hardly supports the proposition that Congress delegated to the federal courts power to alter process in order to provide for what Marshall saw as that "return to ancient usage, and just as well as wise principles" temporarily departed from in the states.

Even granting Senator Rowan's understanding of congressional intent, however, Marshall may have continued to hold both to his decision and the theory supporting it. For Marshall does not say that

Congress actually delegated power for purposes of restoring "ancient usage," he rather proceeds as if he were compelled to construe congressional intent as aimed at such restoration irrespective of what he might have known the facts of congressional intent to be. Marshall says that deviations in the states were contrary to the spirit of the Constitution "and, consequently, with the views of the government," and that "it was proper to provide for that return"; that "Congress, probably, conceived that this object would be best effected" through delegation to the courts; that Congress "could not have intended" to sanction state proceedings, and "therefore" delegated power with the aim of having them changed. The argument is one of identifying proper constitutional principles first, and then concluding that Congress could not have intended otherwise. The sole evidence for congressional intent, in other words, seems to be the propriety of the principles cited. With this language Marshall may have suggested that courts may direct their judgments of congressional intent less by the actual intent of Congress than by their own estimates of what Congress ought to have intended in the public interest.

In tracing the full implications of *Wayman* v. *Southard* it must be observed that in this case Marshall speaks as more than a judicial officer of independent constitutional status with powers, prerogatives, and obligations of his own. Marshall also speaks in this case as an agent of Congress—thereby suggesting the possibility that all agents of Congress may be guided by what, in effect, are extra-statutory standards. If agents of the legislature may be guided by their own judgments of the public interest, may we conclude that Congress may delegate to its agents the power to act in accordance with their independent conceptions of the public interest? Such a doctrine cannot be dismissed as a possibility in this case, given Marshall's constructive understanding of congressional intent. According to Marshall, Congress intended the restoration of certain principles. But Congress made no specifications in the statute concerning the principles intended. The statute identified only the agents in whose hands the task of restoration was entrusted. If those agents, *as agents,* are free to act in accordance with their own conceptions of a just restoration, Marshall might have been prepared to suggest that Congress may delegate the power so to act.

Thus Marshall's opinion in *Wayman* v. *Southard* is open to a range of interpretations stretching from the permissibility only of narrowly circumscribed delegations to the virtual abdication of congressional power to agencies believed better equipped to find and realize the public interest. The facts of the case before him did not require decision in terms of the expansive dicta near the close of his opinion. From the criteria of permissible delegations being applied in this study, it would have been sufficient to show that the delegation at the time of passage of the Process Act did not represent an effort by Congress to evade politically salient issues. As argued by Senator Rowan and as indicated in the early part of Marshall's argument, Congress appears to have intended only the delegation of power to effect technical and relatively noncontroversial adaptations of state process. Marshall could have upheld the delegation as a delegation of ministerial power without suggesting more. Of course, Marshall and the senator would have disagreed strongly on whether the district court's action was within the scope of a delegation of power over mere details. Marshall gave the appearance of contending that the district court's action was ministerial to what Congress had intended—but not without providing a full reconstruction of congressional intent for those who knew better.

The delegation which actually took place was constitutional because there is no evidence that Congress attempted to pass the burden of politically salient decision to the courts. But the action of the district court was not a ministerial act pursuant to a congressional choice concerning the constitutionality or justice of state process. The legality of the district court's action will remain an open question here. The putative delegation in Marshall's opinion could have tended toward constitutionality had Congress in some open, publicly accessible fashion stated its purposes similar to the way in which Marshall tried to reconstruct them. Marshall was wrong about the actual congressional intent. Had he been correct, then it would have been plausible to maintain that Congress had intentionally authorized the action of the district court. A provision for review and reenactment of rules made under the putative delegation would have settled the question of constitutionality in that Congress would have expressed a willingness eventually to choose between the conflicting policies at stake in the process dispute. As it stands, the putative delegation was unconstitutional. Had the actual delegation conformed to Marshall's reconstruction of it, it would have been an unconstitutional evasion of congressional responsibility.

A few other features of *Wayman* v. *Southard* deserve brief mention in advance of later cases. This case could have established the delegability of major decisions in federal constitutional law. Probably one of the factors in its failure to do so was the theoretical cogency of Marshall's argument about filling up details—an argument which, as applied by Marshall to the instant facts, is rather patently out of place. The legacy of the case for future patterns of judicial decision is reminiscent of the legacy of *The Brig Aurora:* an unrealistic conception of the scope of the principle of nondelegation in the major premise, and in the minor premise a fictionalized rendition of the facts at hand. Other features of *Wayman* v. *Southard* to reappear in future decisions include the judicial provision of legislative purposes unexpressed in the statute and broad statements of legislative policy under which power could be delegated.

The Modern Doctrine:
Delegation with Standards

At the turn of the century, despite the growing practice of upholding transfers of power in state and federal courts, judicial doctrine had yet to arrive at the admission that some delegations of legislative power were constitutional. The old approach involved rationalizing delegations in terms of filling up details and finding facts for the suspension or enactment of predetermined legislative policy. Not all of the decisions of the nineteenth century employed the old approach. We have seen that *Wayman* v. *Southard* was quite modern in some of its techniques, and at least one state court would have virtually destroyed the practical effect of the rule by holding constitutional the transfer of any power which was legally recoverable by the legislature.[56] Despite deviations, however, the predominant approach was to uphold delegations by labeling them as narrowly ministerial in one way or another. Jaffe distinguishes a new approach which began to appear in Supreme Court opinions with *Butterfield* v. *Stranahan* (1903)[57] and achieved doctrinal maturity in *J. W. Hampton, Jr. & Co.* v. *United States* (1928), the decision upholding flexible provisions of the Tariff Act of 1922.[58]

In approving a delegation of power to the president to adjust tariff rates up to 50 percent where the president was satisfied that existing rates failed to equalize differences in production costs between the United States and principal competing countries, Chief

Justice Taft stated in *Hampton:* "If Congress shall lay down an intelligible principle to which the person or body authorized to fix such rates is directed to conform, such legislative action is not a forbidden delegation of legislative power."[59] Taft's requirement of an "intelligible principle" became the later requirement for a "reasonable standard" found in the New Deal cases and beyond.[60]

Butterfield v. Stranahan

The facts in *Butterfield* v. *Stranahan* involved a delegation of power to the secretary of the treasury under the Tea Inspection Act of March 2, 1897, to establish minimum quality standards for imported tea upon the recommendation of a board of experts appointed by the secretary. The plaintiff argued that the act was unconstitutional because it attempted to delegate to the secretary "legislative powers which can only be exercised by Congress."[61] The government's response presented the Court with two alternative justifications for the delegation. The doctrinal significance of the case for future developments derives from these alternatives.

The government's first move was to invite the Court to invoke the doctrine of filling up details: it was not legislative power that was delegated to the secretary, said the government, it was a necessary and proper "delegation of details."[62] In its second move the government struck new doctrinal ground with the argument that recent "decisions of this court recognize that to rigidly enforce the doctrine that Congress cannot delegate legislative power would often in effect be a restriction upon legislative power, and they allow Congress very wide latitude in this respect."[63]

The leading citation for the second of the government's arguments was, interestingly enough, *Field* v. *Clark,* even though, as we have seen, *Field* v. *Clark* contained anything but the open call for a liberalized version of the delegation doctrine which we have here in the government's second argument. The delegation of the *Field* case was sustained through a rather strained application of the contingency principle. However, if the citation of the *Field* case here was technically inaccurate, it was apt on other grounds. For if Justice Harlan's opinion in *Field* v. *Clark* proved anything, it proved that new doctrines would be needed for those who would continue to approve delegations of legislative power. By its second argument the government in *Butterfield* was attempting to point the way.

In upholding the provision Justice White stated:

The claim that the statute commits to the arbitrary discretion of the Secretary of the Treasury the determination of what teas may be imported, and therefore in effect vests that official with legislative power, is without merit. We are of opinion that the statute, when properly construed, as said by the Circuit Court of Appeals, but expresses the purpose to exclude the lowest grades of tea... This, in effect, was the fixing of a primary standard, and devolved upon the Secretary ... the mere duty to effectuate the legislative policy declared in the statute. The case is within the principle of *Marshall Field & Co.* v. *Clark* ... we may say of the legislation in this case, as was said in [the Field case] that it does not, in any real sense, invest administrative officials with the power of legislation. Congress legislated on the subject as far as was reasonably practicable, and from the necessities of the case was compelled to leave to executive officials the duty of bringing about the result pointed out by the statute. To deny the power of Congress to delegate such a duty would, in effect, amount but to declaring that the plenary power vested in Congress to regulate foreign commerce could not be efficaciously exerted.[64]

The Court's citation of *Field* v. *Clark* was in error. *Field* was decided through an application of the contingency principle, and *Butterfield* fails altogether to relate the contingency principle. A better citation for the approach in *Butterfield* would have been *Wayman* v. *Southard* in view of the fact that in both opinions Congress was said to have expressed its purposes and to have delegated nonlegislative power. If *Butterfield* contains the emergence in Supreme Court decisions of the modern doctrine of standards, then it is clear that the modern doctrine is an outgrowth of the legislative-details approach. Beyond the fictional part of White's argument leading to the conclusion that the act "does not ... invest administrative officials with the power of legislation," the opinion does well.

The government had cautioned against use of the delegation doctrine in a manner that would actually restrict the exercise of legislative power. We have argued that the scope of the rule of nondelegation should be determined by the idea of constitutional duty. Congress has a duty to choose among the salient alternatives it confronts. When Congress has chosen, it may be compelled to delegate in order to actualize its choices. Justice White undoubtedly went too far when he suggested that Congress should legislate as far as reasonably practicable. But his suggestion implies that Congress has real burdens of choice, and this underlying thought is correct. If we are to follow Jaffe and regard this case as somewhat of a breakthrough in the development of the modern doctrine of delegation with standards, then we can say that the original meaning of the standards requirement was that there had to be discernible legislative purpose behind the delegation. In other words, the problem of statutory standards was originally a problem of legislative decision, not a problem of legislative draftsmanship. The section of the act which delegated power to the secretary did not contain language for the guidance of administrative discretion. The Court found such guidance by looking to other sections of the act and by inspecting the legislative history of the act as reported by the circuit court. This case, extending a technique which appeared in *Wayman* v. *Southard,* may stand for the proposition that sometimes the facts of legislative decision may be enough to satisfy the standards requirement even in the absence of a clear statutory statement of legislative purpose. It is easier to accept this proposition for some cases than it is for others. In this case the absence of a clear statement of policy could not have been the basis for doubt as to what the policy really was, for Congress could hardly have intended anything but the exclusion of substandard tea. In other cases, as we shall see, the absence of clear policy statements can amount to evasions of the responsibility for decision.

As for an evaluation of the delegation itself, the record contains no evidence that Congress delegated for purposes of evading choice between salient political alternatives. The bill occasioned no debate in the Senate and such minimal debate in the House that it is difficult to detect an articulate basis for opposition.[65] In the House the bill was defended as a mere improvement in techniques for enforcing a basic policy adopted by Congress in 1883.[66]

J.W. Hampton, Jr. & Co. v. United States

The Supreme Court's decision in the *Hampton* case upheld the flexible-tariff provision of the Tariff Act of 1922, and upheld it unanimously despite grave questions of constitutionality. Given the kind of discretionary authority delegated to the president, the ambiguity in the language of the statute, and the confusion in the legislative history of the act, the unanimous concurrence in Chief

Justice Taft's opinion indicated a judicial propensity to manipulate well-rehearsed formulas for upholding delegations of any kind. This case caps what Pritchett has termed "a century of judicial rationalization of legislative delegation," following which "there was a widespread assumption that this area was one of the dead letters of American constitutional law."[67]

Section 315 of Title III of the act provided in part as follows:

(a) That in order to regulate the foreign commerce of the United States and to put into force and effect the policy of the Congress by this act intended, whenever the President upon investigation of the differences in costs of production of [American- and foreign-made] articles . . . shall find it thereby shown that the duties fixed in this act do not equalize the said differences in costs of production in the United States and the principal competing country he shall, by such investigation, ascertain said differences and determine and proclaim the changes in classifications or increase or decrease in any rate of duty provided in this act shown . . . necessary to equalize the same. . . . Provided, that the total increase or decrease of such rates of duty shall not exceed fifty per centum of the rates specified in Title I of this act, or in any amendatory act. . . .

(c) That in ascertaining the differences in costs of production . . . the President, insofar as he finds it practicable, shall take into consideration (1) the differences in conditions of production, including wages, costs of material, and other items in costs of production of such or similar articles in the United States and in competing foreign countries; (2) the differences in the wholesale selling prices of domestic and foreign articles in the principal markets of the United States; (3) advantages granted to a foreign producer by a foreign government, or by a person, partnership, corporation, or association in a foreign country; and (4) any other advantages or disadvantages in competition.

Investigations to assist the President . . . shall be made by the United States Tariff Commission . . . and no [presidential] proclamation shall have been issued under this section unless such investigation shall have been made. The commission shall give reasonable public notice of its hearings . . . and . . . reasonable opportunity to parties interested . . . to be heard.[68]

Chief Justice Taft's first step in upholding the delegation was to point out that cost equalization was the legislature's purpose in the flexible-tariff provision and that while cost equalization may have been "difficult to fix with exactness," that purpose was "perfectly clear and perfectly intelligible" on the face of the statute.[69] From the perspective of our analysis, this is the proper approach to the delegation problem in this case. Clearly the flexible-tariff provision of the 1922 act vested the president with extensive discretionary powers, even to the point of practically rewriting sections of the act through the power to change statutory classifications. However, as the delegation doctrine is understood here, the degree of discretion exercised by an agent of Congress is secondary in significance to the question of congressional intent and resolve in making the delegation. Following a proper beginning, the chief justice's opinion continues in an interesting way. At first he appears to lapse into the familiar rationalizations of the delegation decisions. Citing *Butterfield* and other cases, he approvingly notes delegations to executive officers "to secure the exact effect intended" by a statute through "directing the details of its execution."[70] Citing *Field* v. *Clark,* he suggests that the flexible-tariff provisions of 1890 and 1922 "did not in any real sense invest the President with the power of legislation" because the president "was the mere agent of the law-making department to ascertain and declare the event upon which its expressed will was to take effect."[71] In addition to citing traditional formulas, however, Taft seemed to blend them into a more general and permissive formula which was grounded in the proposition that Congress may delegate power, however understood, so long as its choices and purposes are clear. The essence of his own contribution may thus be found in the following:

Congress . . . should exercise the legislative power, the President . . . the executive power, and the courts . . . the judicial power, and in carrying out that constitutional division . . . it is a breach of the national fundamental law if Congress gives up its legislative power and transfers it to the President or to the judicial branch, or if by law it attempts to invest itself . . . with either executive power or judicial power. This is not to say that the three branches are not coordinate parts of one government and that each in the field of its intended duties may not invoke the action of the two other branches in so far as the action invoked shall not be an assumption of the constitutional field of action of another branch. In determining what it may do in seeking assistance from another branch, the extent and character of that assistance must be fixed according to the common sense and inherent necessities of the governmental coordination.[72]

As for the application of this thinking to the instant facts, the chief justice concluded that

> If Congress shall lay down by legislative act an intelligible principle to which the person or body authorized to fix such rates is directed to conform, such legislative action is not a forbidden delegation of legislative power. If it is thought wise to vary the customs duties according to changing conditions of production at home and abroad, it may authorize the Chief Executive to carry out this purpose.[73]

Taft's opinion thus ambiguously straddled the old and new approaches to the problem of upholding delegations of legislative power. It is possible and perhaps desirable to interpret his argument in this case as designed to subsume the familiar approaches under a rule of reason in delegation cases. Although not always followed in subsequent cases, the *Hampton* opinion pointed the way to analyzing delegations less in terms of what kind of power was being exercised by the delegatees and more in terms of congressional intent and resolve. If we overlook his suggestions on filling up details and finding facts, Taft's opinion exemplifies what our analysis indicates is the preferred approach.

Aside from the virtues of Taft's opinion, its basic factual premise —that Congress intended a policy of cost equalization—is questionable. On the surface of Section 315 Congress had provided an intelligible statement of legislative purpose, and the chief justice went no further for his evidence of congressional intent. However, John Day Larkin has argued that the language of the statute was little more than a device for diverting judicial attention from a real purpose of delegating undefined powers for executive use in furthering the protectionist aims of the statute.[74]

Taussig wrote that the rates of the act of 1922 were "higher than any in the long series of protective measures" commencing with the act of 1890. The general fear of a postwar slump, feelings of nationalism engendered by the war, the desire for self-sufficiency in war-related products, the desire for protection among depression-ravaged western farmers, and the rout of the Democrats in the election of 1920—these were some of the factors which "led to an extreme of protection which few had thought possible."[75] The strong protectionist policy of the act was reflected in the inclusion, for the first time in the history of tariff legislation, of language (in Section

315) which openly provided for the protection of American industry without pretending to be raising revenue as a primary object.[76] When the flexible-tariff provision of Section 315 originally came from the Senate Finance Committee in the form of an amendment to the House bill, cost equalization was not the statutory standard. Instead of directing the president to ascertain the "differences in cost of production," as required in the final language of the act, the original proposal spoke of the "difference in conditions of competition in trade." A subsequent amendment by Chairman McCumber of the Finance Committee deleted the words "in trade" in subdivision (a) and added to subdivision (c) what was finally to appear as subsection (4).[77] The president was thus to alter certain rates in accordance with the "difference in conditions of competition" (subdivision [a]) and to ascertain those differences by considering such different production conditions as wages and material costs, wholesale selling prices, and, finally, "any other advantages or disadvantages in competition." This last clause was to appear in the final bill as Section 315 (c) (4). This section and the original standard in subdivision (a) were to cause doubt as to the extent that transportation costs could be a factor in presidential rate adjustments. This doubt was never really clarified by Congress, and the problem was delegated.[78]

Wisconsin's Senator Lenroot, arguing for tighter statutory language, contended that under the "condition of competition" standard, the president was left at liberty to consider internal and external transportation costs at will. With an eye to further protection for domestic manufacturers, Senator Lenroot proposed to substitute the "cost of production" standard for the original "condition of competition" standard.[79] Larkin reports that the Finance Committee accepted this change primarily because it had been convinced that tighter language was needed for the courts, but that there was no agreement in the committee as to what the new language was to mean in practice. The new standard was either "to be construed liberally . . . so that it would amount to the same as 'conditions of competition'; or it was to equalize 'the differences in costs at home and abroad' with all carrying charges not incidental to fabrication omitted."[80] Larkin adds that there is reason for believing that most of the members of the committee accepted the narrow standard on the assurance that it would be liberally construed as well as for the sake of judicially adequate specificity. The committee added the power to consider "any other advantages or disadvantages" in order to insure the possibility of presidential discretion beyond the supposed limits of the cost-equalization standards.[81] Given the subsequent administration and interpretation of the act, Larkin concludes that, instead of cost equalization, the real purpose of the provision was to empower the president "to make such changes as would offset any kind of advantages (whether political or economic) which the foreign producers might enjoy . . . the stated rule, 'cost of production,' served more as a legal decoy than as a yardstick."[82]

Larkin gives an additional reason for believing that cost equalization was not the real policy behind the flexible-tariff provision. He notes that because almost all international trade is predicated on differences in production costs, a true cost-equalization policy for dutiable items would amount to an embargo on most items not on the free list, and while the statutory rates often approach a practical embargo, "they are not all such as to protect the domestic producers against all relevant factors in competition." Nor could they be, given the need for revenues which the tariff still served and the need for partially manufactured goods and raw materials for domestic factories. Larkin cites import figures which show that "the same measure of protection is not accorded all items on the dutiable list," the reason being that "Congress has deliberately set up varying standards." The fact that Congress did not establish a consistently applicable cost-equalization standard for the dutiable list is seen also in several of the statutory rates. The dollar-per-gallon rate on beer, far in excess of production costs, served the policy of prohibition, and the rate on certain coal-tar products was enacted with an eye to developing certain infant industries for the sake of military self-sufficiency. Larkin concludes that "the figures . . . show that Congress intended to produce varying results—that instead of having only free goods on the one hand and well-protected goods on the other, there were to be some rates designed for revenue purposes and others for a measure of protection which was to be less extreme."[83]

We need not discuss Larkin's subsequent points on the consequences of the ostensible standard for the administration of the act. It is perhaps enough here to relate his view that the cost-equalization standard made "absolutely impossible" the task of administration and placed the Tariff Commission "in the midst of constant controversy."[84] All that we need to emphasize here is Larkin's view of a disjunction between the cost-equalization standard and the less rigid, more varied protectionism which actually motivated the act. If the statutory standard in fact deliberately failed to reflect the actual choice made by Congress, and if there was among the supporters of the act a feeling that the actual level of choice was too general to provide a basis for constitutional delegation, then we must incline toward the conclusion that the delegation was unconstitutional. Congress either failed openly to assume responsibility for its actual policy or failed to make what many of its members felt was the necessary discrimination among the salient alternatives facing it.

While these considerations may incline towards a conclusion of unconstitutionality, at least two additional complications suggest the wisdom of leaving the question open. To begin with, it is difficult to escape the cogency of the court's view that Congress should be free to provide for "changing conditions of production at home and abroad." Congressional effort to provide for those conditions through a formula which failed to express its true level of decision may have been influenced by a pattern of judicial decision over which Congress had no direct control. Congress may have chosen to fictionalize its own behavior because of its perception of current judicial doctrine. Had judicial doctrine been more realistic, perhaps a statutory standard could have been found which better reflected the actual congressional policy. But this more accurate standard would have reflected what in reality was a level of decision less specific than the fictional policy of cost equalization. And a statute whose standard accurately expresses the level of decision may nevertheless be unconstitutional because of its failure to reflect a requisite level of discrimination among competing alternatives. Congress, after all, was not free to say, "We cannot decide the question of transportation costs; we openly assume the responsibility of delegating that decision to the Commission and the President."

According to our analysis, however, Congress would have been free to say, "We cannot decide at this time; experiment so that we might decide in the future." A commitment to review and to reenact might have satisfied the constitutional requirement imposed by the nondelegation doctrine as interpreted here. This brings us to the second reason for withholding judgment on the constitutionality of the flexible-tariff provision, the periodic revision of tariff acts which had been traditional in American politics. At the time Congress delegated discretion to the president it could expect to review his decision in about six years, the average interval of the seven major tariff acts in the preceding forty-year period being five and a half years. In the case of presidential revisions of the 1922 tariff, Congress embodied most of them in the congressional act of 1930.[85]

Panama Refining Co. v. Ryan

In 1935 the Supreme Court decided two challenges to the National Industrial Recovery Act of 1933, *Panama Refining Co. v. Ryan*[86] and *Schechter Poultry Corp. v. United States.*[87] Given the extent of judicial permissiveness in delegation cases up to that point, the government did not take the delegation question seriously when it was raised in the *Panama* case.[88] Justice Jackson reported that the delegation question "was so little anticipated that the government's brief of 227 pages and 200 more of appendix devoted only 13 pages to the subject."[89] To the amazement of the nation, the Court sustained the delegation challenge in *Panama,* and four months later in *Schechter* invalidated the central provisions of NIRA, partly on delegation grounds.

In the *Panama* case the Supreme Court for the first time applied the rule of nondelegation to invalidate a congressional delegation of power. The provision in question was Section 9 (c) of Title I of the NIRA, which authorized the president, in part,

to prohibit the transportation in interstate and foreign commerce of petroleum and the products thereof produced or withdrawn from storage in excess of the amount permitted . . . by any state law or valid regulation or order prescribed thereunder.[90]

Speaking for an eight-man majority, Chief Justice Hughes declared this provision unconstitutional primarily because he could not discern in the language of Section 9 (c) or its statutory context a declaration of policy for the guidance of presidential discretion.[91]

Citing the vesting provision of Article I and the necessary and proper clause, Hughes stated that Congress "manifestly is not permitted to abdicate, or to transfer to others, the essential legislative functions with which it is thus vested." However, he recognized that,

legislation must often be adapted to complex conditions involving a host of details with which the national legislature cannot deal directly. The Constitution has never been regarded as denying to the Congress the necessary resources of flexibility and practicality, which will enable it to perform its function in laying down policies and establishing standards, while leaving to selected instrumentalities the making of subordinate rules within prescribed limits and the determination of facts to which the policy as declared by the legislature is to apply. Without capacity to give authorizations of that sort we should have the anomaly of a legislative power which in many circumstances calling for its exercise would be but a futility.[92]

Nevertheless, he quickly added that

the constant recognition of the necessity and validity of such provisions, and the wide range of administrative authority which has been developed by means of them, cannot be allowed to obscure the limitations of the authority to delegate, if our constitutional system is to be maintained.[93]

As for the "limitations of the authority to delegate," the chief justice cited the usual cases and reiterated the legislative-details and contingency arguments.[94] Basically, he assumed that unless Congress established statutory guidance, the president's discretion would be uncontrolled and, therefore, inappropriate for an executive officer. At one point Hughes seemed to say that the delegation of uncontrolled discretion was improper because uncontrolled discretion was a legislative prerogative.[95] He thus appeared to decide the issue in terms of a description of the power exercised by the president, the congressional agent in this case. On balance, however, the language of the opinion eventually amounted to an admission that Congress may delegate discretionary functions so long as those delegations are accompanied by one or another form of congressional guidance.

The point on which the question of constitutionality turned is revealed in the lone dissent, Cardozo's:

My point of difference with the majority of the court is narrow. I concede that to uphold the delegation there is need to discover in terms of the act a standard reasonably clear whereby discretion must be governed. I deny that such a standard is lacking in respect of the prohibitions permitted by this act when the act with all its reasonable implications is considered as a whole.[96]

Looking to the "whole structure of the statute," Cardozo found that the president was to prohibit the shipment of the oil when in his judgment the prohibition would "effectuate the declared policies of the act . . . announced by section 1 in the forefront of the statute as an index to the meaning of everything else that follows."[97] Section 1 declared in part that it would be the policy of Congress

to remove obstructions to the free flow of interstate and foreign commerce which tend to diminish the amount thereof . . . to eliminate unfair competitive practices, to promote the fullest possible utilization of the present productive capacity of industries, to avoid undue restriction of production (except as may be temporarily required), to increase the consumption of industrial and agricultural products by increasing purchasing power, to reduce and relieve unemployment, to improve standards of labor, and otherwise to rehabilitate industry and to conserve natural resources.[98]

This was the very language which Hughes and the majority had dismissed as too broad to be regarded as anything more than merely introductory to the act.[99] The majority held the language of Section 1 to "contain nothing as to the circumstances or conditions in which transportation of petroleum . . . should be prohibited—nothing as to the policy of prohibiting, or not prohibiting.[100] Cardozo maintained in reply that the Court should construe the act to mandate prohibition of the oil shipments upon presidential findings that such shipments defeated the policies of Section 1. Cardozo was thus prepared to treat as a statement of statutory conditions what the majority was willing to view only as a general and preambulatory expression of statutory ends.[101] To the majority Cardozo's approach was an "effort by ingenious and diligent construction to supply a criterion" for prohibiting the oil shipments—a fruitless effort since it "still permits such a breadth of authorized action as essentially to commit to the President the functions of a legislature rather than those of an executive or administrative officer executing a declared legislative policy."[102] Cardozo in turn insisted that if the delegation were not regarded "an instance of lawful delegation in a typical and classic form . . . categories long established will have to be formulated anew."[103]

As the justices perceived it, the issue concerned the status as legislative guidelines of the policy aims in Section 1. Were these expressions specific enough to guide executive discretion? Were they consistent with each other? Could they be made consistent in light of a more general policy implicit in the act? Did the Court have an obligation to formulate a more general standard and construe the exrpessed aims and processes of the act as details pursuant thereto? Did the standards and methods of delegation in Section 1 conform to patterns of delegation which the Court had upheld previously? As the justices understood the delegation problem, these were the issues before them. From the frame of analysis here, on the other hand, the constitutionality of the delegation in Section 9(c) would normally depend on the related but distinguishable question of whether Congress delegated in order to evade decision between alternatives which were salient at the time of delegation.

However, before turning to the question of congressional resolve relative to Section 9(c), the effects of another section on the constitutional question should be noted. For no matter how the question of congressional resolve is answered, Title I of the Recovery Act contained an explicit guarantee either of expiration or of legislative review and reenactment. As the delegation question is conceived in this study, this guarantee should have insulated all sections of Title I from declarations of unconstitutionality on delegation grounds, including Section 3, voided in *Schechter*. Mandatory expiration or legislative review was insured through Section 2(c), which declared that

> This title shall cease to be in effect and any agencies estab-
> lished hereunder shall cease to exist at the expiration of two years
> after the date of enactment of this act, or sooner if the President
> shall by proclamation or the Congress shall by joint resolution
> declare that the emergency recognized by Section 1 has ended.[104]

Because of Section 2(c), the Court could have interpreted Title I as an effort to develop mature legislation through a period of administrative experimentation. While trial and error may be and, in the case of NIRA particularly, has been called an irresponsible method of policy formation, from the perspective here the Constitution sanctions it.[105] Section 2(c) should have saved the entire title. Let us, however, evaluate Section 9(c) as if the provision for expiration in 2(c) had not been present in the act.

The early part of Justice Cardozo's dissent suggests that the purpose of Congress in Section 9(c) was to give the federal government some power to help the states ameliorate the demoralizing overproduction of oil.[106] The floor debate on 9(c) supports this suggestion, as congressional controversy and decision clearly focused on the problem of overproduction.[107] While congressional intent was reasonably clear, however, the question raised by the Court's majority still stands: if Congress had intended to mandate the prohibition of the so-called "hot-oil" shipments, then why the permissive delegation to the president? Congress redrafted the act after *Panama* in order to satisfy judicial objections. The floor debate on this second effort brings out the significance of the permissive delegation in the original act. It appears that the original delegation was permissive because Congress wanted to provide some means for inhibiting the states from inflating the price of oil through the imposition of unreasonable production restrictions.[108]

The permissive delegation in 9(c) meant that federal restrictions on interstate shipments of hot oil could be suspended or applied by the president as he thought necessary to help maintain what he regarded as a fair price for oil and oil products—and this without any statutory guidance on what the price of oil and oil products should be. Congress was unable to provide such guidance because, as we shall see, a major area of congressional irresolution in the attempt to develop a recovery policy had been the question of basic pricing policy for industry as a whole.

When 9(c) was enacted there was little question that twenty-five cents per barrel of crude oil was destructive of the industry's small, independent producers. But if twenty-five cents per barrel was demoralizing, by what policy was a fair price to be determined? Was the test to be the level at which a certain competitive situation within the industry could be maintained? If so, then here too the failure of Congress to provide a standard can be traced to another of the unresolved problems of the recovery act: the nation's basic policy toward competition. The permissive delegation in 9(c) pointed beyond the immediate problem of overproduction in oil to the underlying problem of a basic recovery policy. And Congress itself undermined Cardozo's constructive understanding of 9(c) when, upon reenactment, it provided both a mandate provision and a permissive provision, separating them with the intent of leaving the mandate provision intact should the permissive provision be invalidated.[109]

Had the original delegation in 9(c) simply mandated the prohibition of hot-oil shipments, the delegation would have been valid. But, because Congress had not intended a simple prohibition of such shipments, and because, as we shall see, the basic policy underlying the act was left in doubt, the guarantee of review in Section 2(c) was the only thing that could have saved Section 9(c).

Schechter Poultry Corp. v. United States

The *Schechter* case is the most famous of the New Deal delegation decisions. Here a unanimous court declared Section 3 of the NIRA an unconstitutional delegation of congressional power. Chief Justice Hughes, speaking for the Court, followed the doctrines and techniques developed in *Panama* to find that Congress had failed to perform its "essential legislative function" of establishing "the standards of legal obligations."[110] Cardozo concurred, holding that, if the delegation were upheld, "anything that Congress may do within the limits of the commerce clause for the betterment of business may be done by the President upon the recommendation of a trade association by calling it a code. This is delegation running riot. No such plenitude of power is susceptible of transfer."[111] While the *Schechter* decision has its critics, it enjoys a much higher level of approval than the decision in *Panama*.[112]

In part, Section 3 of Title I read as follows:

(a) Upon the application to the President by one or more trade or industrial associations or groups, the President may approve a code or codes of fair competition for the trade or industry or subdivision thereof . . . if the President finds (1) that such associations or groups impose no inequitable restrictions on admission to membership therein and are truly representative . . . and (2) that such code or codes are not designed to promote monopolies . . . and will tend to effectuate the policy of this title: *Provided*, that such code or codes shall not permit monopolies or monopolistic practices. . . .

(c) After the President shall have approved any such code, the provisions of such code shall be the standards of fair competition for such trade or industry or subdivision thereof. Any violation of such standards . . . shall be deemed an unfair method of competition within the meaning of the Federal Trade Commission Act, as amended; but nothing in this title shall be construed to impair the powers of the Federal Trade Commission under such act, as amended.[113]

In searching for a standard the chief justice found "fair competition" unacceptable. It did not refer to a "category established in law" to be used as a limitation on the making of codes. It was to be used instead as a "convenient designation for whatever set of laws the formulators of a code for a particular trade or industry may propose and the President may approve . . . as being wise and beneficient provisions for the government of the trade or industry in order to accomplish the broad purpose . . . stated in the first section of Title I"[114] Hughes thus construed the idea of "fair competition" in Section 3 with the "general aims" of Section 1 which he had declared inadequate as a basis for delegating power in *Panama*.

In view of Cardozo's dissent in *Panama*, there was not great clarity in his concurrence in *Schechter*. Had the general aims of Section 1 been adequate as standards for the permissive delegation regarding interstate shipments of hot oil, then why were they unsatisfactory as limitations on the code-making authority? Cardozo's concurrence did not explain this inconsistency. He attempted to explain his objection to the code-making authority by contrasting it with the FTC's authorization to investigate and eliminate "unfair methods of competition." The power of the FTC was "negative," he said, and had the codes of "fair competition" in the recovery act been defined as codes eliminating "unfair methods of competition," he would have upheld the delegation.[115] "But," said Cardozo,

> there is another conception of codes of fair competition, their significance and function, which leads to very different consequences. . . . By this other conception a code is not to be restricted to the elimination of business practices that would be characterized by general acceptance as oppressive or unfair. It is to include whatever ordinances may be desirable or helpful for the well-being or prosperity of the industry affected. In that view, the function of its adoption is not merely negative, but positive; the planning of improvements as well as the extirpation of abuses. What is fair, as thus conceived, is not something to be contrasted with what is unfair or fraudulent or tricky. The extension becomes as wide as the field of industrial regulation.[116]

In the *Panama* opinion Hughes had pointed out that Congress had not mandated the interception of hot-oil shipments as an unfair method of competition.[117] The delegation in Section 9(c) was thus termed by the chief justice a permissive delegation, and he argued that if approved "there would appear to be no ground for denying a similar prerogative of delegation with respect to other subjects of legislation" or to all subjects of legislation.[118] Cardozo attempted to deny that the delegation in 9(c) was as permissive as claimed by the Court. His first effort was to argue the judicial propriety of construing the statute as if hot-oil shipments had been proscribed as unfair methods of competition.[119] Unable to maintain this position in the face of statutory language, Cardozo finally settled on the argument that although there was no compulsory interdiction of hot-oil shipments, Section 1 provided adequate standards for limiting executive discretion. Evaluating those standards in view of Cardozo's subsequent classification in *Schechter*, we see that they are both "positive" and "negative" and that Cardozo was forced into selecting as his "ultimate" standard in *Panama* the broad, positive goal of "industrial recovery."[120] Cardozo's *Panama* opinion comes to imply that executive discretion in hot-oil shipments is limited by judgments as to what promotes "industrial recovery." Without attempting to criticize the distinction between positive and negative standards, we see that Cardozo found a positive standard acceptable in *Panama* but refused to approve a positive standard in *Schechter*.

Cardozo's distinction between positive and negative standards fails as a test for deciding when a delegation is "unconfined and vagrant." Of course, the delegation in Section 3 was vastly greater than the delegation in 9(c). But the scope of the latter was more limited only because there was both a more specific designation of subject matter (hot oil versus the competitive practices of the nation's industry) and a more restrictive specification of means (regulating the flow of hot-oil shipments versus prescribing codes of fair competition). Although he did not articulate a theory that relatively high specificity in means and subject matter are adequate substitutes for clear statements of contingencies and policies,[121] this generalization can be extracted from Cardozo's arguments. Such a rule neither flows from nor is compatible with the rule of nondelegation as conceived in the present analysis. The question in every case should be whether Congress has delegated as a means to pursuing policy or as a way of evading responsibility for decision. How this question is affected by statutory specificity in subject matter and means cannot be determined without knowledge of the intentions of Congress relative to salient policy alternatives.

With the possible exception of the labor standards of Section 7, the act said little about what constituted "codes of fair competition." The principal statutory guide to what should have been in the codes was the statement of goals in Section 1, and, as we have seen, the ultimate standard implicit in Section 1 was that of "industrial recovery." Let us therefore investigate the nature of the decision to delegate for that end. Was this an act of irresolution on the part of Congress?

The Roosevelt administration began to develop its recovery plans following the president's dissatisfaction with a Senate-passed thirty-hour work bill in April 1933, designed to share the available work among a larger number of workers. Within days after the president's call for a substitute, Labor Secretary Perkins submitted several proposals to Congress, including wage and hour provisions which brought immediate protests from the business community. With the aid of General Hugh S. Johnson, later to be named the Recovery Administration's first director, Assistant Secretary of State Raymond Moley had begun investigating the proposals of business leaders. Their initial proposal called for suspension of the antitrust laws, presidentially sanctioned business agreements concerning competition and labor practices, and federal licensing to insure compliance. Another group, headed by Senator Robert Wagner, emphasized public works, industrial loans, and governmental sanction of trade-association agreements. A third group, under the leadership of Commerce Undersecretary John Dickenson, proposed trade associations as instruments of national planning. By early May these proposals had distilled into two major drafts, and under presidential pressure a bill including most of the early proposals, with the principal exception of industrial loans, went to Congress with a presidential demand for immediate action. In less than six weeks the administration had formulated its recovery proposal.[122]

The bill seemed to contain something for everyone. Business spokesmen were praising devices that could be used to stop competitive price-cutting, unfair trade practices, and overproduction. Labor welcomed the guaranteed right to organize and bargain collectively. Social reformers pointed to the means for eliminating substandard working conditions and child labor, and economic planners stressed the prospects for a rational economic order cognizant of its social responsibilities.[123] Ellis Hawley argues, however, that the popularity of the bill was partly a reflection of the fact that Congress, "by a resort to vagueness, ambiguity, and procrastination," had, in effect, "refused to formulate a definite economic policy or to decide in favor of specific economic groups."[124] Satisfaction with the particulars of the measure disguised conflicting beliefs as to what the act would do, for the bill had embodied conflicting theories of economic recovery. Hawley describes these theories in general terms as "a belief, on the one hand, that by raising wages, spreading work, and holding down prices, total purchasing power could be expanded; a belief, on the other, that by checking destructive competition and insuring profits, business confidence could be restored and new investment spending stimulated."[125]

This conflict of theories was to be expressed in the need to find a middle way between what General Johnson and the business community typically termed "destructive competitive practices," price slashing below costs being the most conspicuous example, and what adherents to the antitrust tradition typically called "monopolistic practices," which for some of them included any act of price-fixing by industrial agreement.[126] The nature and extent of price-fixing to be permitted thus became a critical problem. Congress confronted the question but could not answer it. The final draft of the bill revealed the irresolution by exempting the codes from the antitrust laws in Section 5 after providing against "monopolies and monopolistic practices" in Section 3. The resolution of the question was delegated to the administrators of the act.

Immediately upon commencement of debate in the House in late May doubts were expressed by those for and against the bill concerning the nature and extent of price-fixing to be permitted. Speaking for the bill, Congressman Doughton of North Carolina justified the ambiguity as one of those "flexible remedies . . . always necessary in emergencies . . . which the President may use to prevent monopoly on the one hand and ruinous competition on the other."[127] Representative Cox, a Georgia Democrat who was to vote against the bill, insisted on knowing whether the bill amounted to a "price fixing scheme."[128] Not all who supported the bill were willing to give a straightforward answer to this question.

Vinson of Kentucky attempted equivocal denials of price-fixing throughout the debate[129] while Cellar of New York admitted the possibility from the beginning and called for candor from the bill's supporters. "Is there any question," Celler demanded, "but that those agreements that may be entered into by trade groups may provide for the fixing of prices?" "You must have price fixing," he concluded, "otherwise you destroy the purpose of the bill."[130] Doughton, pulling back from Celler's candor, set the tone for much of the remainder of the debate with a warning that "chatter and hair-splitting about the Constitution will find little sympathy among the American people. They trust our President."[131]

In addition to protesting the threat of price-fixing, the bill's House opponents attacked on delegation grounds. Cox anticipated some of the *Schechter* opinion by distinguishing the delegation in the Recovery Act from previous ones to the ICC and other agencies. "Here," he said, "no rule is laid down by Congress to guide the President. The exercise of the powers delegated is conditioned upon no fact, is consent upon the happening of no event, but is an unconditional grant to be exercised at will and as the President might elect."[132] Instead of attempting to meet this argument on its own premises, the bill's supporters inclined towards the demurrer that the act was necessary as a temporary measure in a serious national emergency.[133] One of the supporters was compelled to assert that "under normal conditions this bill would not pass this Congress" because it gives "entirely too much power to ... one man." Yet, concluded Glover of Arkansas, "in this emergency we must trust the President."[134] The House passed the bill by a three-to-one vote on May 26.[135]

Senate approval was not achieved as easily. Senator William E. Borah of Idaho and a group of antitrusters including Senators Burton Wheeler, Hugo Black, and Huey Long contended with Senator Wagner on the significance of suspending the antitrust laws. The antitrusters charged that the act would open the way to price fixing, restraint of trade, and a system of monopolies.[136] Wagner insisted that while sales below costs might be forbidden as a move to end cutthroat competition, the kind of price fixing which could bring about a system of monopolies would not be sanctioned by the act.[137] The anitrusters responded that it would not be possible to restrain business from monopolistic price fixing, once the Sherman Act was suspended, unless such practices were explicitly prohibited. Wagner, who had his own fears about uncontrolled price fixing,[138] finally agreed to accept an amendment by Borah which provided that no code should "permit combinations in restraint of trade, price fixing, or other monopolistic practices."[139] With this amendment the Senate passed the bill by a vote of 58 to 24.[140]

But the Borah amendment was not to survive. Appearing before the conference committee, General Johnson argued that the Borah amendment would nullify the act. As he was to recall his argument, Johnson reasoned that if it were true that acts of price fixing and combination in restraint of trade were monopolistic in themselves, "NRA had better be abandoned," because "every code is a combination in restraint of trade," including those containing "agreements against child labor and sweat shops,"[141] and because at least one form of price fixing, that preventing "predatory price slashing," was actually a means of preserving the competitive system.[142] Business leaders demanded defeat of the Borah amendment, arguing that suspension of antitrust laws was their due "in consideration of decreased working hours and increased wages" granted labor by the act.[143] Wagner, "upon further study" of the implications of the Borah amendment, gave the conferees a substitute which struck all mention of the words "price fixing" and "restraint of trade" and provided simply that the codes "should not permit monopolies or monopolistic practices."[144] The conference committee accepted the substitute.

The conference report was accepted by the House on June 10 over the muffled protests of the antitrusters that the Wagner substitute was "quite a little coming down" from the Borah amendment.[145] In the Senate, Senator Black argued that what he perceived as the difficulties of calculating cost-of-production figures and the inevitable monopolistic price fixing whenever "a number of men engaged in manufacturing are permitted to get together in a room and discuss anything with reference to their business" should have compelled Congress to make a clear choice between meaningful alternatives instead of trying "to straddle the fence." "Our trouble," said Black,

> is not in the problem of production but results from improper and unfair methods of the distribution of our products. Without expressing any view at this time as to which is to be preferred, the continuation of the competitive system to regulate prices or the system of governmental regulation of prices and profits, let us face the situation squarely and adopt one or the other; and when the conferees, if they should come back—which they may not— should continue to adhere to the abandonment of the competitive system by striking out the amendment of the Senator from Idaho to preserve the competitive system, let them substitute something of

some kind or some character that will prevent the fixing of prices by monopoly.[146]

But the conference report passed the Senate unaltered.

Congress thus refused to develop a clear-cut policy on the price problem, and "the conundrum of price," as Schlesinger has termed it, was to plague the administration of the act from the beginning to the end of its life.[147] Immediately upon the enactment of the act, President Roosevelt, joined by General Johnson, proclaimed a moratorium on price increases "as long as possible." But less than a week later Johnson retreated before the strong demands of the trade associations and announced that the codes might include agreements prohibiting price cuts below production costs.[148] As Johnson's attention focused more on what Schlesinger calls the drama of code-making than on the content of the codes themselves, Johnson became the most visible defender of the price and production controls which found their way into the codes.[149]

Conflict grew between Johnson and other administration insiders as the latter began to demand government price fixing in the face of what they saw as monopolistic price fixing by the trade associations.[150] Roosevelt sided with Johnson, but, as prices continued to rise, sources within the NRA itself began to condemn the agency as the breeder of monopoly.[151] Johnson, with some minor concessions, resisted the antitrusters while exhorting business to keep prices down. But prices continued to rise and with them the protest over NRA policy.[152] Finally, in May 1934, Roosevelt yielded to growing pressure from congressional and administrative sources and appointed a cabinet committee to study the implications of price policy.[153] Towards the end of the month Johnson limited price fixing only to "emergencies" to be ascertained by NRA economists for critical cases and then only for ninety-day periods.[154] But the reaction of business was so intense that Johnson qualified the new policy into practical insignificance and moved the NRA into a position of stalemate which lasted through Johnson's resignation in late August and through two presidential reorganizations until the agency's demise at the hands of the Court in late May 1935.[155]

On the relationship between what he terms the initial act of congressional buck passing and the act's administrative history, Hawley says,

The very nature of the act made internal dissensions among its administrators virtually inevitable. In practice the NRA became a mechanism that conflicting groups sought to use for their own ends, an agency that was unable to define and enforce a consistent line of policy; and in this welter of conflict and confusion, it was scarcely surprising that the result turned out to be . . . an "administrative, economic, and political mess."[156]

The decisions of *Schechter* and *Panama* were not to provide future events with an effective rule of law, although no delegation since has equalled the scope of the Recovery Act. In *Carter* v. *Carter Coal Co.* (1935),[157] the Court invalidated sections of the Bituminous Coal Conservation Act of 1935 partly because a delegation of rule-making powers over hours and wages to groups of private producers and miners was declared "legislative delegation in its most obnoxious form; for it is not even delegation to an official or an official body, presumptively disinterested, but to private persons whose interests may be and often are adverse to the interests of others in the same business."[158] The Court held the delegation offensive to the due process clause of the Fifth Amendment.[159] Without attempting to evaluate the due process argument or other parts of the decision further, we can say that the application of our criteria need not have had the same result. From our perspective, that is, from the logic of the delegation doctrine alone, if Congress delegates as an instrument of decision, the delegation is constitutional regardless of the agent's status—just as the agent's status will not save a delegation designed to evade responsibility. Certainly, we can disagree with the possible suggestion that a given delegation is less objectionable depending on the agent's status. It is at least arguable that the presumed disinterestedness of public officials depends on their identities as parts of a constitutional system of offices and powers. If that system is altered by delegation or other means the presumption of disinterestedness may be defeated. Such would appear to be compatible with the teaching that a system of checks and balances can substitute for the virtue of officials.[160] In any event *Carter* was the last time the Court used the delegation doctrine to invalidate an act of Congress.

Since that time, delegations approved by the Court have been extensive. In *United States* v. *Rock Royal Co-op.* (1939),[161] the Court upheld a delegation under the Agricultural Marketing Agreement Act of 1937 to the secretary of agriculture to maintain the price of certain agricultural commodities at levels of purchasing power for a specified base period as long as those levels were approached "by gradual correction of the current level at as rapid a rate as the Secretary . . . deems to be in the public interest and feasible in view of the current consumption demand."[162] The Court found congressional standards adequate despite Justice Roberts's comments that the "supposed standards . . . are themselves so vague . . . that neither [the secretary] nor anyone can accurately apply them," thus rendering clear "the unlimited nature of the delegation."[163] Roberts dissented again when the court upheld in *Yakus* v. *United States* (1943),[164] the Emergency Price Control Act of 1942, which authorized a price administrator to fix prices for commodities, rents, and services which "in his judgment will be generally fair and equitable and will effectuate the purposes of this act."[165] Roberts maintained that the purposes of the act were too broad to place any limits at all on the discretion of the administrator, and that there was "no doubt" that the standards requirement of *Schechter* was being overruled in silence.[166] Other delegations followed and were upheld against attacks that they were too broad and discretionary, including a delegation in the Renegotiation Act of 1942 to renegotiate defense contracts yielding what the statute referred to simply as "excessive profits."[167]

The continuation of such permissive holdings into the postwar period has caused some commentators to suggest that the delegation doctrine is entering a new phase in which the requirement of legislative standards is being dropped. Woll suggests that "reasonably definite jurisdictions" and standards emanating from the agencies themselves may be replacing the requirement of clear statements of legislative intent.[168] Jaffe indicates some concurrence in this view,[169] and Davis has put part of it into a proposal for revitalizing the delegation doctrine.[170] The emerging phase can trace its judicial origins to opinions by Justices Cardozo and Stone. We have already noted the implication in Cardozo's *Panama* dissent that a narrow definition of subject matter can partly compensate for a clear statement of legislative policy with respect to that subject matter.[171] Jaffe has discovered Stone's suggestions in *Yakus* that the adequacy of a legislative standard may rest in part on how well its definition is developed by those who are to administer it.[172] We have stated that from the perspective of our analysis narrow definitions of subject matter are no substitute for clear statements of policy. However, Jaffe's comment on Stone's suggestion indicates clearly how the emerging doctrine could be related to our criteria. The suggestion that standards emanate from the agencies themselves, says Jaffe, "may appear irrelevant to the question whether Congress *has* adequately spoken; but it is relevant to subsequent control by the courts, by the public, and once more by the Congress."[173]

We noted in Chapter 2 a class of cases in which the Court attempts to invalidate or narrow by construction overly broad legal standards administered in a manner threatening protected individual rights.[174] The Court has moved against such provisions as one that empowered a state board to deny motion picture permits for films deemed "sacrilegious,"[175] one that authorized a police chief to issue permits at his discretion for sound-amplification devices,[176] and one that authorized a congressional committee to conduct wide-ranging investigations into "un-American" activities.[177] One such case, *Kent* v. *Dulles* (1957),[178] has attracted attention in recent years as a resurrection of the delegation doctrine. Here the Court narrowly construed the scope of a delegation in order to avoid constitutional questions concerning restrictions on the right of Communist party members to travel abroad, citing as it did the standards requirement of the *Panama* case, among other things. But despite the *Panama* citation, this case has all the appearances of an effort to protect rights of free movement, association, and belief. It is not a case seeking to hold Congress to some conception of its constitutional responsibilities.

Kent v. *Dulles* concerned applications for passports denied by the secretary of state on grounds of alleged Communist party association. The secretary acted under an act of 1952 which made passports necessary for foreign travel and left their issuance to his discretion. The Court recognized the constitutional strength of the "freedom of movement," and the real question of the case was the extent to which this freedom could be abridged on national security grounds. However, the Court avoided the constitutional question by interpreting the statute to narrow the secretary's discretion to considerations which raised no serious constitutional issues. This was done by asserting that the act of 1952 incorporated prior administrative practice which had "jelled" to authorize restrictions only on grounds of citizenship or allegiance and unlawful conduct, neither of which had been asserted here. Explicitly excluding "problems that may arise under the war power," the Court then said, "Since we start with an exercise by an American citizen of an activity included in constitutional protection, we will not readily infer that Congress gave the Secretary of State unbridled discretion to grant or withold it."[179]

This language would be enough to indicate that the basis of the decision was a desire to protect the freedom of movement. But then the Court added almost immediately that if the freedom of movement "is to be regulated, it must be pursuant to the law-making function of the Congress.... And if that power is delegated, the standards must be adequate enough to pass the accepted tests," citing *Panama* and others at this point.[180] It would be a mistake to take this dictum as indicating probable approval of the restrictions had they issued from Congress and not from the secretary of state. The Court did not call for greater specificity of decision or for finer legislative draftsmanship as means of holding the secretary responsible to congressional policy. Indeed, the opinion for the four-man minority shows that through legislative and administrative history congressional authorization for the secretary's restrictions could have been found easily had the majority been so disposed.[181] But the delegation problem was not the majority's real concern. Soon after citing *Panama,* the majority concluded:

> To repeat, we deal here with a constitutional right of the citizen, a right which we must assume Congress will be faithful to respect. We would be faced with important constitutional questions were we to hold that Congress ... had given the Secretary authority to withold passports to citizens because of their beliefs or associations. Congress has made no such provision in explicit terms; and absent one, the Secretary may not employ that standard to restrict the citizens' right of free movement.[182]

Mora v. McNamara

The Joint Resolution of Congress of August 10, 1964, supporting United States participation in the defense of South Vietnam, the so-called Tonkin Gulf Resolution, has been the subject of the most serious delegation debate of the cold war period. The nation was in the midst of the presidential campaign of 1964 when, on August 3, the administration announced that on the previous day North Vietnamese gunboats had attacked an American destroyer on patrol in the Gulf of Tonkin off North Vietnam. Following a second attack on August 4, President Johnson addressed the nation as "President and Commander in Chief" and announced a series of retaliatory air strikes against gunboat ports and supporting facilities in North Vietnam.[183] With assurances that "our response, for the present, will be limited and fitting," that we were engaged in merely "limited military action," and that we "still seek no wider war," the president informed his radio and television audience that

> I have today met with the leaders of both parties in the Congress ... and I have informed them that I shall immediately request the Congress to pass a resolution making it its determination to take all necessary measures in support of freedom and in defense of peace in Southeast Asia.
>
> I have been given encouraging assurance by these leaders ... that such a resolution will be promptly introduced, freely and expeditiously debated, and passed with overwhelming support. And just a few minutes ago I was able to reach Senator Goldwater and I am glad to say that he has expressed his support of the statement that I am making to you tonight.[184]

Thus, in a presidential call for an expression of national unity in the face of allegedly "open aggression on the high seas against the United States of America,"[185] the Tonkin Resolution was conceived.

Congress was quick to grant the president's request. On August 5 a resolution went to Congress, stating, in part, that (1) "Congress approves and supports the determination of the President, as Commander in Chief, to take all necessary measures to repel any armed attack against the forces of the United States and to prevent further aggression," and (2) that consonant with the Constitution and its treaty obligations, "the United States is ... prepared, as the President determines, to take all necessary steps, including the use of armed force, to assist any member or protocol state of the Southeast Asia Collective Defense Treaty requesting assistance in defense of its freedom."[186] On August 7, by a vote of 82 to 2, the Senate adopted the resolution, as did the House on the same day by a vote of 416 to 0.[187]

At the time the resolution was adopted in the summer of 1964 the most important issue was whether the legislative and executive branches of the government would present a solid front to North Vietnam.[188] Despite the warnings of Senators Morse and Gruening to consider the resolution as a grant of unlimited authority to wage war,[189] a show of unity at a time of crisis seems to have been uppermost in the minds of most congressmen. Indeed, there was some feeling that an expression of unity was necessary in order to avoid the actual use of the power to wage war, the power whose delegation Morse and Gruening were advising against.[190] However, as events brought the president to the realization that American forces would have to assume the major burden of honoring the commitment to South Vietnam, some of those who opposed a widening of the war began to view the Tonkin Resolution as an unconstitutional delegation of congressional war powers.[191]

In written testimony before the Senate Judiciary Subcommittee on the Separation of Powers in the summer of 1967,[192] Senator Fulbright, contrary to views he had expressed three summers before, attacked the Tonkin Resolution as a "blank check ... piloted through the Senate with ... undeliberate speed ... giving away ... that which was not ours to give."[193] "The war power," he added "is vested by the Constitution in the Congress, and if it is to be transferred to the Executive, the transfer can be legitimately effected only by constitutional amendment, not by inadvertency of Congress."[194] The transfer of power in the Tonkin Resolution was hardly an act of "inadvertency," as we shall see, but it was a "blank check" of sorts and, as such, a delegation whose constitutionality is legitimately questioned.

The Supreme Court declined an opportunity to hear and decide the constitutionality of the Tonkin delegation in *Mora* v. *McNamara*[195]. Over the dissents of Justices Douglas and Stewart, the Court denied certiorari in a dismissal of a suit for a declaratory judgment that United States military activity in Vietnam was illegal. Although we do not have the benefit of a decision on the merits, Justice Stewart's dissenting opinion offers a useful framework of questions for discussing the delegation question and, incidentally, for identifying the limits of that issue on the overall question of the war's constitutionality. Justice Stewart felt that the Court "should squarely face" the following "large and deeply troubling questions":

I. Is the present United States military activity in Vietnam a "war" within the meaning of Article I, Section 8, Clause 11 of the Constitution?

II. If so, may the Executive constitutionally order the petitioners to participate in that military activity, when no war has been declared by the Congress?

III. Of what relevance to Question II are the present treaty obligations of the United States?

IV. Of what relevance to Question II is the joint Congressional ("Tonkin Bay") Resolution of August 10, 1964?

(a) Do present United States military operations fall within the terms of the Joint Resolution?

(b) If the Joint Resolution purports to give the Chief Executive authority to commit United States forces to armed conflict limited in scope only by his own absolute discretion, is the Resolution a constitutionally impermissible delegation of all or part of Congress' power to declare war?[196]

The answers to all of these questions are beyond the purposes of this study as is, therewith, a judgment on the legality of the American action in Indochina as such. The concern here is to evaluate the constitutionality of the Tonkin Resolution as a delegation of power, not to judge the constitutionality of the war itself. The two questions are related, as Justice Stewart's opinion shows, but they are also independent of each other in view of the possibility of concluding on the one hand that the delegation was unconstitutional but on the other that the war itself was constitutional. The latter conclusion is at least possible because the war might be viewed as a legitimate exercise of the president's power as commander in chief.[197] Thus, when Congress voted to repeal the Tonkin Resolution in the summer of 1970, President Nixon did not oppose this action. The State Department had informed Senator Fulbright in the spring that it held the resolution dated by events and that "The Administration is not depending on any of these resolutions as legal or constitutional authority for its present conduct of foreign relations, or its contingency plans."[198] The administration maintained this position even after the Cambodian action of April 1970,[199] an action which the president took as commander in chief without prior congressional authorization of any kind. As long as the scope of presidential power as commander in chief remains a controversial matter, as it shall remain here, no inferences as to the constitutionality of the war can be made from the constitutional status of the resolution. The interest here is in the delegation question only (Stewart's question IV[b]), and other questions will be approached only to the extent that they bear on that question.

From our perspective the constitutionality of the Tonkin Resolution as a delegation of power rests on the nature of the choice which Congress can fairly be said to have made at the time of the resolution's adoption. If the resolution followed upon and expressed with relative specificity a choice between the salient policy alternatives facing Congress at the time, then the resolution is constitutional as a delegation. If, on the other hand, the resolution delegated the choice among salient alternatives to the President, it is unconstitutional as a delegation. Whether Congress understood the resolution to be a delegation, however, is itself problematic as an aspect of the unanswered questions concerning the scope of the president's power as commander in chief. In other words, it is possible that Congress may have construed the resolution as a statement approving and supporting the president in decisions which were presumed to be constitutionally within his prerogatives. If so, then Congress should not be charged with having deliberately "given away" anything. As we shall see at a later point in this discussion, the question of how Congress perceived the war powers of the Constitution at the time the resolution was adopted complicates the constitutional status, as a delegation, of the resolution itself.

If we assume (and below we shall examine this assumption) that Congress intended not only to approve exercises of presidential power but also to authorize action which it thought constitutionally impermissible otherwise, then the resolution should be adjudged an unconstitutional delegation of power. If Congress understood itself to be delegating something, then the Tonkin Resolution fails our criteria because Congress knowingly left unsettled the general scope and character of the military action it was authorizing. The record shows, first, that Congress was aware of a certain number of policy alternatives in Indochina; second, that the commitment of Congress to some of those alternatives was a matter of reasonable doubt; third, that Congress was aware that the language of the resolution was broad enough to authorize alternatives which extended beyond the point of reasonably settled congressional commitment; and, finally, that Congress declined to adjust the language of the authorization to the actual level of decision. Those alternatives which were clearly subjects of congressional indecision were thus knowingly delegated to the president. As we shall see, there were very good reasons for such a delegation under the circumstances, but such delegations are unconstitutional nevertheless.

Proceeding on the assumption that the Tonkin Resolution was understood by Congress as, in part, a grant of power to the executive to take steps which he could not lawfully take in the absence of the grant, we have first to enumerate what Congress saw as the alternative kinds and degrees of military involvements in Indochina. The floor debate indicates that, among the greater number of alternatives which could have been discussed, the members of the House and Senate were concerned principally with the following.

At one extreme, war with China was regarded within the serious possibilities, particularly by Senator Morse who, in his speech against the resolution on August 5, appears to have felt that, relative to U.S. military involvement, China and North Vietnam could be considered a unit.[200] A second, more probable and thus more frequently mentioned, course was an all-out commitment of U.S. forces in the North.[201] A third altenative, more properly treated as a group of possibilities, was that of "limited" involvement.[202] To some this meant ground and air defense in the South with retaliatory air strikes in the North;[203] to others it meant defense in the South with preventive air strikes in the North and neighboring countries.[204] Among the other limited-war alternatives can be listed what Senator Morse saw as the bluff of a large buildup in the South and a threat to expand to the North in hopes of causing a Communist retreat from the South.[205] These and other limited-war alternatives were compounded by the question of whether the United States was prepared to assume the main burden of ground action if that was necessary to defend the South.[206] And, finally, there was Senator Morse's proposal that the United States disengage its military assistance altogether and work through the United Nations to restore peace in the area through the Geneva agreements.[207]

Of these four general alternatives—war with China, war with North Vietnam, limited and essentially defensive action concentrated in the South, and a military withdrawal coupled with a reliance on diplomacy—the bulk of congressional opinion probably favored the third. In view of the North Vietnamese actions, the president's retaliatory response thereto, and the president's appeal for an expression of unity, Senator Morse's proposal was unacceptable to almost everyone at that particular time. Senator Church probably spoke for both friend and critic of our Indochina policies when he said, "There is a time to question the route of the flag, and there is a time to rally around it, lest it be routed."[208] On the other hand, no one seemed willing to call openly for the pursuit of either of the first two options.[209] A few voices in both houses berated our allegedly no-win policy in Indochina, decried our tolerance of privileged sanctuaries, and expressed the hope that the Tonkin retaliations signaled a basic change in policy.[210] But no one was prepared to propose all-out war in the North. The president had assured them that we were engaged in "limited military action" and that we "still seek no wider war," so most congressmen supported an uncertain middle way.

Not only was there an absence of expressed support for an all-out commitment in the North, there was, especially in the Senate, substantial sentiment against it.[211] Early in the Senate debate Senator Fulbright gave what he regarded as the relationship between the president's retaliation and the commitment to some form of limited war:

> This action is limited, but very sharp. It is the best action that I can think of to deter an escalation or enlargement of the war. If we did not take such action, it might spread further. If we went further and ruthlessly bombed Hanoi and other places, we would be guilty of bad judgment, both on humanitarian grounds and on policy grounds, because then we would certainly inspire further retaliation.[212]

The effect of the President's retaliation as a deterrent to a wider war was a point frequently maintained in both houses, as was its corollary, that Congress could contribute to the deterrent through a show of unity with the president.[213] This theme was prominent enough in both houses to indicate significant opposition to an all-out effort in the North and beyond. At best, congressional commitment to the first two of the general alternatives sketched above was a matter of reasonable doubt.

However, despite reasonable doubt whether Congress would have committed itself to the more extreme alternatives beyond some version of the limited-war position, the language of the resolution authorized in advance whatever future course the president might want to take—including all-out military operations against North Vietnam and even China. Congress, moreover, was aware of the potentially extreme scope of the resolution, and Senator Fulbright, who openly opposed the exercise of some of the options admittedly within the language of the resolution, refused nevertheless to reduce its scope. Throughout debate in the Senate, and to a lesser degree in the House, there were apprehensive remarks about the relatively extreme scope of the resolution. Responding to such a remark by Senator Brewster, Fulbright stated that he would "look with great dismay on a situation involving the landing of large armies on the continent of Asia." While agreeing with Brewster, "that that is the last thing we would want to do," Fulbright recognized that "the language of the resolution would not prevent it." "It would authorize," he said, "whatever the Commander in Chief feels is necessary."[214] Fulbright responded similarly to other senators and seemed content to rely on the provision of the resolution reserving the power to terminate by a concurrent resolution which the president did not have to approve.[215]

Senator Nelson, even though he was to vote for the resolution, was more insistent on an effort to specify its outer limits. On August 7, after expressing "great confidence in the President" but lamenting "the differing interpretations which have been put upon the joint resolution with respect to what the sense of Congress is," Nelson proposed an amendment which read in part as follows:

> The Congress . . . approves . . . the President's declaration that the United States, seeking no extension of the present military conflict, will respond to provocation in a manner that is 'limited and fitting.' Our continuing policy is to limit our role to the provision of aid, training assistance, and military advice, and it is the sense of Congress that, except when provoked to a greater response, we should continue to attempt to avoid a direct military involvement in the Southeast Asian conflict.[216]

Fulbright rejected the opportunity to clarify the scope of the resolution according to Nelson's proposal, despite his professed view that the Nelson amendment was in line with what he approvingly understood the president's policy to be. "I do not object to it as a statement of policy," Fulbright said,

> I believe it is an accurate reflection of what I believe is the President's policy, judging from his own statements. That does not mean that as a practical matter I can accept the amendment. It would delay matters to do so. It would cause confusion and require a conference, and present us with all the other difficulties that are involved in this kind of legislative action.[217]

Obviously, delay and restrictive clarification would have depreciated the value of the resolution as the expression of unity so urgently requested by the president.[218] Fulbright might have agreed with the additional point by Congressman Hosmer on the same day that the president's retaliatory air strikes and the ensuing congressional resolution, while commendable, would still leave difficult decisions of policy unresolved, and correctly so: "It is incumbent upon the President," said Hosmer, "to make less clear to the Communists in Peiping just what our intentions are unless these decisions are to be made much more difficult."[219] Fulbright himself was to suggest later that one of the justifications for the "discrepancy between the language of the resolution and the intent of Congress" was the greater deterrent potential in language which could be interpreted as advance congressional consent "to a full-scale war in Asia should the President think it necessary."[220]

Thus did Congress delegate beyond its level of relatively clear decision—knowingly and even rationally, if unconstitutionally.

The conclusion that the Tonkin Resolution was an unconstitutional delegation of power is based in part on the assumption that Congress understood the resolution to be legally necessary for an expansion of our military involvement in Indochina. Unless Congress understood itself to be giving something away, the delegation question as conceptualized here is simply irrelevant to any questions about the constitutional status of the resolution. As noted above, the act uppermost in congressional minds in August 1964, was a show of national unity in a time of crisis.[221] It appears likely that Congress did not understand itself to be *authorizing* anything, so much as it was *approving* and *supporting* actions which were seen to be within the prerogatives of the president. It is not clear from the record of the floor debate whether the dominant intention was one of authorization or of approval and support.[222] Senator Fulbright has, on different occasions, interpreted it both ways. After President Nixon signed the repeal of the resolution in January 1971, Fulbright treated the resolution as authorization for the war in order that he might argue that Congress had the authority to bring the war to an end through such action.[223] In an earlier statement intended to deny congressional authorization for what the war had become, Fulbright recalled,

> The prevailing attitude was not so much that Congress was granting or acknowledging the executive's authority to take certain actions but that it was expressing unity and support for the President in a moment of national crisis and, therefore, that the exact words in which it expressed those sentiments were not of primary importance. . . Insofar as the question of authority to commit the country to war was thought of at all, the general

attitude was one of acceptance of the power of the President, in his capacity as Commander in Chief, to commit the armed forces to at least limited war.[224]

The issues of what the actual congressional intention was and what the legal effect of the resolution's repeal ought to have been will not be handled here. They are mentioned here for purposes of showing the limits of the delegation question in this case. Certain things have been assumed here in order to take up the delegation question. Having illustrated the application of the rule of nondelegation to the resolution, if only hypothetically, our purposes have been reached.

Nondelegation and congressional oversight

As the rule of nondelegation has been interpreted in this study, Congress may not deliberately transfer to others the power to decide between the most salient policy alternatives presented to it. However, the rule of nondelegation does not proscribe delegations of discretionary authority intended by Congress as instrumental to its decisions. As long as Congress delegates for purposes of exercising power, the minimal values grounding the idea of nondelegation are served. It may even be argued (with reservations to be noted) that when Congress delegates from indecsion these values may still be satisfied through statutory commitments to decide eventually. Through the use of provisions which result in mandatory review and reenactment of continuing programs, the rule of nondelegation may not be incompatible with congressional use of agencies for generating and experimenting with policy proposals. But, measured by the norms supporting the idea of nondelegation, nothing short of mandatory review will save delegations expressing congressional irresolution.

With the rise of executive discretion and the practice of delegating broad powers, Congress has relied upon several methods short of mandatory review for the control of administrative discretion. These methods include regulating the flow and direction of appropriations, determining the organizational structure and status of administrative agencies, influencing personnel policies and choices, requiring formal congressional clearance of particular administrative decisions, investigating administrative conduct, and interfering in the day-to-day performance of administrative duties on an individual and informal basis. Collectively, these devices are usually referred to as techniques of "congressional oversight," and, although observers vary on their approval of different oversight techniques, the oversight function itself is conventionally seen as necessary for maintaining administrative responsibility to Congress.

The subject of legislative oversight is germane to the present discussion in view of the suggestion by some observers that the techniques of legislative oversight in some manner provide substitutes for congressional adherence to the principles of nondelegation. Thus, commenting on what he terms a "spectacular delegation without any guiding standards" (to apportion water among the southwestern states in time of shortage) Davis finds no reason for prohibiting delegations of such scope. The courts, he says, can effectively review challenges to particular apportionments in the absence of statutory standards through a due process standard of "reasonableness" which "is always present," and

> Congress through its committees and otherwise may keep watch over the Secretary's exercise of power. A committee may require reports, ask questions, make suggestions, apply pressures, manipulate appropriations, threaten legislation withdrawing or altering power, publicize faulty administrative judgments, and through any or all of these weapons it may retain the ultimate control over administrative policies.[1]

The point is made frequently enough elsewhere to warrant brief discussion here. In what respects, if any, are the values supporting the rule of nondelegation served through various forms of congressional oversight? Are these values served completely through the use of any technique short of mandatory review and reenactment? These are the questions of the present chapter.

As we approach an analysis of oversight techniques, it will be helpful to keep in mind the purposes of this study. The relevance here of oversight techniques results solely from the proposition that the use of these techniques is in some way a substitute for adherence to the rule of nondelegation. For this reason our concern with oversight techniques is a rather limited one. The rule of nondelegation and its supporting values will constitute the sole criteria for the present evaluation of oversight techniques. In determining whether it is likely that a given technique can serve the constitutional values served by the rule of nondelegation we shall not be concerned with every way in which the technique could bring about what could be called administrative responsibility to Congress. We shall be concerned with the utility of these oversight techniques in enabling Congress to make authoritative decisions at some point after it has delegated responsibility to others. If, for example, we believed that use of the appropriations process were a substitute for adhering to the rule of nondelegation, we might attempt to show how Congress could have clarified and narrowed its intentions after power was initially delegated to the president in, say, the Tonkin Resolution. To conclude, as we shall, that the various oversight techniques are poor substitutes for the rule of nondelegation is not to measure them by criteria attaching to the other functions legislative oversight might serve. Our treatment of these techniques, both in describing and evaluating them, is governed by our interest in the rule of nondelegation.

The task of identifying appropriate criteria for evaluating oversight techniques as substitutes for the rule of nondelegation begins by recalling the affirmative prescription implicit in the idea of nondelegation: Congress has a duty to decide among the salient policy alternatives presented to it. From a constitutional point of view what we mean by "Congress" and the process of "congressional decision" can in part be determined by consulting the Constitution. The law-making processes in the Constitution should help us find some of the criteria for evaluating new techniques purporting to be substitutes for the old.

Generally, and for purposes of this discussion, we might distinguish two kinds of congressional decision: those aimed at changing the legal status quo and those not aimed at changing it. Decisions not to change the status quo are reached typically by the failure of a legislative proposal for change. Typically, and for our purposes, we can say that Article I requires that both houses of Congress and the president concur in decisions to change the legal status quo. In the presence of a presidential veto, two-thirds of each house must concur. When a decision to change the status quo is involved, neither the House not the Senate alone can speak for Congress. On the other hand, decisions not to change the status quo do not require the same measure of agreement between both houses. Each house can be seen as having an absolute veto on those decisions for change which require the concurrence of both houses. Therefore, we can say that when a decision not to change the status quo is involved, either house can speak for Congress.

From these considerations we are entitled to several general conclusions in advance of an examination of specific oversight techniques. First, oversight techniques employed to narrow the meaning of broad delegations in ways which legally change the status quo existing prior to the delegation should in some way require the affirmative approval of both houses of Congress and the president, or two-thirds of each house in the absence of presidential concurrence. If, for example, we treat the Tonkin Resolution as a delegation of congressional power, then, as we have seen, Congress failed to choose between the salient policy alternatives it considered; the power of choice was delegated to the president. However, Congress may have reserved the right to narrow the meaning of the power delegated, by authorizing only a limited period of presidential action followed by a review of the situation by both houses as a condition for continued action.[2]

A second general implication of Article I for the subject of oversight techniques is that oversight decisions which have the effect of maintaining the legal status quo may be made by either house. In other words, either house may exercise the power to stop proposed changes in the status quo. The 1949 Executive Reorganization Act thus correctly gives to either house the power to veto reorganization plans submitted by the president.[3] However, provisions of the same act raise constitutional questions by permitting a reorganization plan to go into effect if it is not vetoed by either house within sixty days. This provision is suspect in our terms because we cannot always count an act of congressional silence as an act of affirmative congressional decision.

The features of the policy-making process in Article I and their immediate implications constitute the controlling criteria for the evaluation of oversight techniques in this study because they merely index some of the terms of the rule that Congress should decide among salient alternatives. However, these criteria may not be the only ones relevant to our discussion in view of those norms with which the delegation doctrine has been associated historically. A given oversight technique may find approval when measured by our primary criteria but still raise questions on, say, separation of powers grounds. From our perspective criteria drawn from the rule's historical associations are not controlling. Nevertheless, in view of the conventional understanding of the delegation doctrine, criteria of historical derivation may receive some mention, at least. We now turn to those oversight techniques whose use might plausibly serve as substitutes for congressional decision among salient policy alternatives at the time of enactment.

The Legislative Veto

Paraphrasing Joseph P. Harris, the legislative veto as currently practiced may be defined as a statutory device whereby specified administrative decisions are required to be submitted to Congress or to its agents (usually committees or subcommittees) for approval before going into effect. Approval may be by both houses, either house, or by other units (usually committees or subcommittees). Approval may be expressed through failure to veto during a waiting period or through affirmative action. Whatever the congressional agent or the form of approval required, the process does not permit approval or disapproval of administrative proposals with changes in the substance of the proposals and other amendments.[4]

The principal constitutional objections to the legislative veto have been that it is contrary to the law-making process prescribed in the Constitution, that it violates the separation of powers, and that in some forms it delegates to committees, subcommittees, and others, powers which should be exercised by Congress as a whole. These objections can be met only partially, and typically at the expense of values and conceptions logically or historically connected with the rule of nondelegation.

The legislative veto has been thought contrary to the law-making process prescribed by the Constitution for two reasons: first, the veto is not explicitly authorized by the Constitution, and, second, it is held to be an unconstitutional infringement of the president's veto power.[5] The first of these arguments appears the easiest to refute, but from the present perspective it cannot be dismissed entirely. In an influential paper defending the constitutionality of the legislative veto, Joseph and Ann Cooper have pointed out that the law-making process prescribed by the Constitution is not the only process relative to law-making which Congress is authorized to follow.[6] The power to express its opinions through resolutions not subject to presidential veto and the power to conduct legislative investigations are two processes employed by Congress relative to law-making which are not explicitly authorized by the Constitution. Accordingly, the Coopers reason that if Congress

> can act legitimately in a legislative capacity in ways other than those followed in law-making . . . is it then necessarily forbidden to devise new mechanisms and procedures to aid in the performance of its functions merely because these mechanisms are novel or different? As a general proposition, the answer must be no.[7]

Two points may be made in response to this approach. To begin with, the Coopers appear to overlook a practice observable throughout the history of constitutional discussion on the scope and nature of governmental powers: while powers may range and develop much beyond the explicit, the new and novel are generally rationalized in terms of the explicit. New mechanisms and procedures are not *necessarily* forbidden, but in a constitution conceived as a written constitution and as premised on the principle that only granted powers may be exercised, new mechanisms and procedures are inevitably suspect and in need of support in terms of what is written. Second, it is not the relative novelty of the legislative veto on which objections have centered. The problem has not been whether the veto is implicitly authorized, the question has been whether it is implicitly forbidden by prerogatives belonging to units other than those exercising the veto. For example, for those who feel that the Constitution permits legislative change of an administrative interpretation of an act only through new legislation, there could be an implicit prohibition of a one-house veto in the two-house requirement in Article I. It could be argued that one house cannot veto an administrative act because one house cannot pass new legislation. Similarly, an implicit prohibition against any kind of congressional veto can be found in the Constitution's provsion for a presidential veto. Perhaps the question of whether the legislative veto is authorized could have stood by itself, but it has been accompanied by questions of usurpation.

The more serious challenge is that the legislative veto infringes the president's veto power. Again, the assumption in this challenge is that a legislative veto has the effect of changing the meaning of a statute by altering the permissible range of administrative action under the statute. It is thus conceived as a form of legislation. Citing Madison[8] and the language of Article I,[9] Harris argues that the president's veto extends not only to every *bill,* but to all actions of Congress which "have the effect of law."[10] On the other side, the Coopers have cited Story's opinion that the "negative of the President applies only to ordinary cases of legislation,"[11] and the legislative veto, they argue, is not an ordinary act of legislation. They conceive the legislative veto to be "ancillary to legislation and not legislation per se."[12] In reaching this conclusion the Coopers recall the constitutionality of contingent legislation and contend that "conditions stipulated through a (legislative) veto provision are no different than conditions which have been stipulated as precedent to executive action in a number of areas." They add by way of example that "If the findings by the President in the *Hampton* case are not viewed as 'legislating,' even though the act allows the President to rewrite substantially its provisions . . . why then must congressional action through the veto be seen as 'legislating'?"[13]

The Coopers' response is apt as a retort to critics of the legislative veto who insist on permissive interpretations of the Constitution on occasions of power-transfer to the executive and restrictive definitions when power is going the other way. But it hardly satisfies the criteria here. "Legislative," "executive," or whatever, the presidential decision in the *Hampton* case could not have been made directly by Congress without opportunity for presidential approval. However legislative power is defined, it still appears that through the legislative veto Congress and its agents may sometimes reach major decisions of policy without executive concurrence. The feeling that this offends constitutional provisions which give the president a veto over such decisions will probably not disappear through the use of verbalisms.

This is not to say, however, that attacks on the legislative veto might not be softened somewhat under different conceptions of the kind of power being exercised, for the defense of presidential power against the legislative veto may sometimes be premised on less than completely realistic conceptions. Harris attacks the analogy between the legislative veto and contingent legislation with the remark that

It is one thing for Congress to enact legislation which is contingent upon the occurrence of certain events . . . it is quite another for Congress to reserve to itself the right to determine in the future whether an executive decision made in pursuance of law shall be carried out. In one case the condition is external to Congress and its action is complete when legislation is enacted; in the other case the condition involves the future decision by Congress itself, and in a manner not sanctioned by the Constitution.[14]

But is it simply true that in all cases of formal enactment congressional decision is "complete" in terms of decision among actual political alternatives? The principle of nondelegation indicates that formal enactments ought to be complete relative to salient alternatives, but instances of congressional delegation from irresolution indicate that this is not always the case.

If it is appropriate to speak of delegations from congressional irresolution as incomplete in some sense, and if through provision for mandatory review and reenactment Congress may be viewed as having delegated the development of viable policy proposals through periods of experimentation, then there may exist a class of enactments which could be interpreted as deferrals of legislative action rather than legislative action in a decisive sense. The legislative veto under this class of enactments need not be interpreted as depriving the president of his right to veto, since the presidential veto is not used until the legislature has acted. When the realities behind a formal enactment represent a deferral of legislative action, a legislative veto of administrative proposals could stand in principle as a rejection of a proposed change in the status quo, and the veto of the president would not be a necessity in such instances. Thus, the presidential veto would be bypassed only in cases of congressional approval of proposals submitted by agents other than the president. Negative congressional decisions in this type of enactment would present no threat to the presidential veto since, even here, there is no change in the status quo; positive decisions would represent such a threat. And the threat to the president's veto could be removed altogether by recognizing the president's right to veto agency proposals approved by less than two-thirds of both houses of Congress.[15]

This conception may be somewhat less artificial than that proposed by the Coopers,[16] but it fails to remove other constitutional objections to the legislative veto. Giving the legislature power to disapprove administrative proposals after the enactment and before the formal repeal of statutes which authorize such proposals can be challenged as interference with powers vested in administrative agencies by the separation of powers.[17] To such objections the Coopers have replied, in effect, that if distinctions relative to the separation of powers are ineffectual as restrictions to the growth, through delegations, of executive power, they should not be any more restrictive when relative increases of congressional power are at issue. Indeed, argue the Coopers, turning the tables completely, to be more restrictive in the latter case than in the former would weaken prospects for restoring an equilibrium of power essential to the separation of powers.[18] But here, again, the Coopers either depreciate or obfuscate distinctions associated with the delegation doctrine—and without removing the impression that decisions after enactment and before repeal concerning the meaning of a statute belong to agents other than the legislature. Perhaps the best that we could hope for would be to quiet that impression somewhat with the argument that, as with the presidential veto, the occasions for executive and judicial functions relative to statutes do not occur until after legislative decision is made. But this may not take us very far either, for it would still seem that we should be entitled to count formal enactment as decision.

Third, when Congress delegates a veto to either house, a committee, subcommittee, state or private agency, the veto itself is vulnerable to objections on delegation grounds.[19] Again, it can be said to these objections that if Congress may delegate to executive agencies, it may delegate to other agencies. It may also be said that delegations to other agencies are ancillary to legislation, not legislation per se, that they are as legitimate as other congressional practices ancillary to legislation. We have seen, however, that rationalizations of this character are not satisfactory in the present context. If the delegation of a veto can be understood as an instrument of decision among salient alternatives, the delegation doctrine is not offended. However, in the absence of decision, the delegation of a veto power is as offensive as any other delegation, except perhaps for delegations, under certain conditions, of the power to negate proposed changes in the status quo. When Congress delegates as a substitute for decision, nothing less than action by both houses and the president can change the legal status quo in a manner compatible with the values supporting the delegation doctrine.

Finally, we must note that even if it is conceptually possible for specific instances of the legislative veto to satisfy the minimal criteria of the delegation doctrine, the legislative veto as a congressional practice cannot be an adequate substitute for the *rule* of nondelegation. The reason lies in the restrictions placed on congressional power to amend agency proposals by current conceptions of the legislative veto. To the degree that the legislative veto cannot be used to amend administrative proposals, congressional power to choose between policy alternatives cannot be as great in decision by veto as it is in decision by statute. Of course, we can conceive of cases where all of the existing alternatives can reasonably be formulated in terms of accepting or rejecting an administrative proposal. But for most cases and in principle Congress does not have the options through the veto that it would have through statute. At best, therefore, the legislative veto can substitute for adherence to the rule of nondelegation only in limited classes of cases.

The Appropriations Process

The appropriations process provides Congress with several instruments for adjusting and sharpening the operational meaning of broad delegations in light of changing circumstances and perspectives. Administrative options can be influenced through the selective application of money to advance or impede different operations, policy-oriented personnel requirements, statutory provisos, and informal, nonstatutory, instructions during the hearings, in the subcommittee reports, and on the floor. From our perspective the appropriations process has the advantage of a process with clear constitutional credentials providing annual review and involving both houses of Congress and the president. But the formal aspect of the appropriations process is significantly limited in its capacity for substantive change in existing law,[20] and the use of informal means for this purpose offends several values associated with the delegation doctrine. On balance, this most powerful of oversight techniques cannot provide positive direction of policy in a manner free of constitutional difficulties, and it fails as a substitute for the prescriptions of the delegation doctrine.

The limitations of the appropriations process as an instrument for narrowing broad delegations of power stem from the nature of the process itself. Although jurisdictional friction between legislative and appropriations committees indicates that the line separating their functions is not always clear,[21] a basic distinction exists between authorization and appropriation—"between the passage of acts which define purposes, convey power, and authorize appropriations, on the one hand, and the year-by-year provision of money, on the other."[22] This distinction is reflected in the rules of both houses which provide, basically, that funds may not be appropriated in authorizing bills, and appropriations bills may not include legislation.[23] More specifically: (1) appropriations bills may not direct administrators to do anything unless authorized by law; (2) appropriations bills may not change existing law by adding to it or repealing it; (3) affirmative directions for administrators may not be issued in appropriations bills—even when authorizing bills grant discretionary authory to administrators; (4) administrative discretion may be restricted only through simple prohibitions on the use of appropriations; and (5) limitations in appropriations acts may not impose new duties on an administrator.[24]

These requirements are not without ambiguities and loopholes, and the rules have been evaded in the statutes. Nevertheless, except in the House, under special rules waiving points of order, any member may challenge attempts to include legislation in appropriations bills, and this threat deters such attempts.[25] The principal means of evading the rules are not their ambiguities and loopholes, but the informal, nonstatutory aspects of the appropriations process. For the rules cripple the formal process as an innovative, positive and comprehensive policy device.

At every stage of the appropriations process subcommittee members and others interested in a given program will attempt to make a record for guiding administrators in the affirmative ways prohibited for the bill itself by the rules. The first opportunity for nonstatutory direction occurs in the subcommittee hearings. Subcommittee members are eager to state for the record their suggestions and admonitions to administrators and to bring administrators into verbal agreement on specifics.[26] The record made during the hearings becomes a supplement for the interpretation of the subcommittee's report. The subcommittee report is the most important instrument of nonstatutory control.[27] The report is the product of the subcommittee chairman and the assistant clerk, written sometimes in consultation with departmental budget officers. It is rarely altered by the full committee or the house itself, although it is subject to debate and its provisions may be defeated through amendments to the bill, disagreements between houses, and conflict with the conference report.[28] The report usually contains the positive mandates, suggestions, and advice forbidden by the rules in the bill itself, along with strictures, threats, and admonitions.[29] Among directives in the report which would be out of order for the bill one might find the initiation of new programs, reorganization requirements, requests for investigation of problems, instructions relative to specific problems, and interpretations of authorizing statutes.[30] The authority of the report is maintained by the threat of reductions in appropriations the following year.

Members not on the subcommittees seek to affect the meaning and status of provisions appearing in the report by making a record during the floor debates. The techniques employed vary from leading questions asked for purposes of "clarification" to compliments and other expressions of support for the subcommittee's work and threats to transform provisos in the report into formal amendments. Floor debate is carefully read by administrators who are seeking to determine the degree of support for language in the reports.[31] Following passage of a bill, efforts at control continue through informal communications between administrators and legislators. These "interim supervisory relationships," as Macmahon terms them,[32] provide opportunities for continuous oversight and adjustment by the subcommittees and for agency appeals from the nonstatutory instructions and restrictions in the reports (normally to subcommittee chairmen and ranking members).[33]

Michael Kirst evaluates these devices favorably for their superiority to statutory techniques in the positive control of substantive policy and for their utility in reconciling what he sees as the values of increased legislative involvement in administration and increased administrative flexibility.[34] He also feels that the value of whole-house control is served better through nonstatutory than through statutory devices. Decentralization of decision-making to the subcommittee level is most pronounced in the appropriations process, and gathering support for amendments to overcome committee recommendations is an unusually difficult matter. Kirst reasons that because of the norms favoring committee domination of the formal process, the broader participation possible in the informal process brings it closer to whole-house control.[35] However, he also recognizes that because the committee reports may not be amended and because neither of the full chambers is kept informed of the interim changes in nonstatutory controls worked out largely between agency representatives and subcommittee leadership, the value of whole-house control, even as he defines it, is not served completely by the informal devices.[36]

Whatever the comparative merits of the informal process from other perspectives, it fails when measured by the norms supporting the rule of nondelegation. The instructions expressed through the informal process, to begin with, are simply not legally binding, and administrators sometimes depart from them in controversial matters.[37] Moreover, the meaning of nonstatutory directives is often unclear, owing to conflicts between different parts of the record for a given act.[38] Also, the duration of nonstatutory directives is uncertain, with effectiveness normally limited to the one-year period of the appropriations cycle. For these reasons, nonstatutory directives cannot always be expected to have the degrees of authority and clarity possible for statutes.[39]

Finally, the informal process has permitted a relatively high degree of subcommittee participation in administrative decisions, raising questions concerning the separation of powers. With the advent of the performance budget and the reduction in the number of items in the appropriations acts, there has been an increase in the number and detail of nonstatutory directives and in the interim adjustments of those directives by subcommittee and agency leadership.[40] Legislators and administrators meet throughout the year on agency requests for such adjustments as transfers among funds earmarked in the reports and changes in funds for specific purposes. Subcommittee chairmen have come to expect that the agencies will consult with them before significant administrative policy is made, and in some cases this clearance procedure has resulted in informal legislative veto.[41] Although nonstatutory control is normally ineffective in the face of policy formulated or strongly supported by the White House, subcommittee efforts at control are persistent.[42] Of course, such practices are open to charges, on grounds of the separation of powers, of legislative encroachment on administration. For these reasons the appropriations process cannot provide a substitute for the delegation doctrine.

Committee Oversight

Committee oversight of administrative activities takes a number of forms including the committee veto, requirements for administrative reporting to committees, requirements for periodic or continuous consultations between agencies and committees, and committee investigations of agency performance.[43] Our interest in these practices is their use as substitutes for procedures prescribed by the rule of nondelegation. If the rule of nondelegation requires that Congress choose among the salient alternatives confronting it, we ask whether the methods of committee oversight can enable Congress to make such choices in a constitutional manner. The rather obvious answer is that committee oversight is constitutional only as a means to statutory decision, not as a substitute for it.[44]

The first set of constitutional objections to a reliance on committee oversight as a substitute for statutory decision has to do with norms derived from the law-making process of Article I. Committee oversight, by definition, is a function exercised by committees; as such it cannot satisfy the norms of full-house, two-house, and presidential concurrence established by Article I for law-making actions. As we have argued, Congress could authorize the committee veto as a substitute for decision under some circumstances, but such authorizations could be used only to disapprove agency proposals. When Congress has deferred decision, a committee veto could prevent administrative action; however, it would not be constitutional for a committee to take affirmative action of a law-making character unless the committee itself could claim to be an agent of Congress operating under a valid delegation of power. Given these conditions, the committee veto can hardly be counted a substitute for the delegation doctrine.

A second set of reasons against the use of committee oversight as a substitute for statutory decision derives from the separation of powers. With the exception of the committee veto, the various forms of committee oversight share with their constitutional prototype, the investigatory power, a foundation in the legitimate need for information.[45] The use of the investigatory and other committee functions for purposes of pressuring administrators into policy alternatives desired either by Congress or by its committees can be attacked as noninformational in intent and, therefore, as encroaching on administrative functions. Harris makes a distinction between "legislative oversight" and "legislative control," the latter referring to "legislative decisions prior to the relevant administrative action," and the former to "review after the fact," including "inquiries about policies that are or have been in effect, investigations of past administrative actions, and the calling of executive officers to account for their financial transactions."[46] In practice the line between oversight and control is not always easy to find,[47] but as a matter of constitutional theory the distinction is clear. Oversight is constitutionally justified as a necessary and proper method of gathering information for purposes of control. When oversight becomes control, objections on separation of powers grounds are in order.

The Concurrent Resolution

Concurrent resolutions are adopted by both houses of Congress and take effect without presidential approval. These resolutions appear to conflict with the provision of Article I that "Every order, resolution or vote to which the concurrence of the Senate and House of Representatives may be necessary ... shall be presented to the President."[48] Cornelius Cotter explains that the exemption of concurrent resolutions from the constitutional requirement is based on the theory that they "are not legislative in nature and have no effect beyond the confines of the Capitol."[49] Cotter notes that while most of these resolutions are of a "housekeeping or purely advisory nature," they have nevertheless been used to influence policy by terminating delegations, enabling administrative action, and approving or disapproving administrative action.[50] Thus the War Powers Act of November 1973, enables Congress to terminate by concurrent resolution presidential commitment of troops abroad prior to the sixty- to ninety-day limit set by the act for commitments not authorized by Congress.

Congress uses the concurrent resolution to terminate programs either by a simple declaration that they are to be terminated or by declaring an end to the conditions on which the continuation of the programs are contingent.[51] The first of these practices can be challenged as an effort to evade the president's right to veto repealing legislation. The second might be attacked as an invasion of administrative functions.[52] Both may be defended as possible instruments of valid delegations under different circumstances, if validity is measured solely by the minimal requirements for a valid delegation. Congress could delegate fact-finding powers to a majority of both houses if such delegations were instruments of statutory choice among salient alternatives. Congress could also delegate to both houses the termination of programs and actions on admitted policy grounds if it could be said that the enabling act intended to develop the material for decision through a period of administrative experimentation. At best, however, these practices would remain constitutionally suspect and limited to comparatively weak forms of control.

As a device for enabling administrative action, no problems would be raised on delegation grounds in cases where presidential action could be interpreted as concurrence in the enabling decision. However, where agencies not under presidential control were involved, an act of enabling without presidential approval, or its legislative equivalent, could be challenged as a violation of the Constitution's executive veto provisions. Therefore, the only way for us to rationalize the concurrent resolution as an enabling device is to suppose it pursuant to a clear policy-choice by both houses and the president (or two-thirds of each house in the absence of presidential approval). In other words, the two houses of Congress must themselves be the recipients of power under a valid statutory delegation of power.

Given these conditions and restrictions, Congress cannot employ the concurrent resolution as a substitute for adherence to the rule of nondelegation.

Review and Reenactment

The techniques of legislative oversight discussed above fail from a constitutional point of view as substitutes for adherence to the rule of nondelegation. As we have interpreted the rule in this essay, Congress may not deliberately pass to others the burden of decision among the salient policy alternatives presented to it. Once Congress has breached the rule against such delegations, recovery completely free of legitimate constitutional objection is possible only through new legislation. Through a permissive interpretation of the delegation doctrine, however, delegations from congressional irresolution could be constitutional—at least when measured by the minimal values supporting the rule—if they could be interpreted as instruments of policy decisions yet to be made. A statutory provision for mandatory review and reenactment could be presumptive evidence that Congress had committed itself to decide eventually the issues delegated. Thus, the section of the NIRA which imposed a two-year time limit might have been used to validate delegations of the act, as we have argued.

We have also suggested here that provisions for mandatory review and reenactment might remove some of the constitutional objections to techniques of congressional oversight. If, for example, Congress is understood to have authorized a period of administrative experimentation preparatory to legislative decision, the legislative veto and the concurrent resolution used negatively may be somewhat less offensive than they are under present conceptions of the separation of powers and the president's right to veto efforts to repeal and amend existing law. Despite these advantages, however, several objections, conceptual and political, would remain to the use of mandatory review and reenactment as a device for saving delegations which would be invalid otherwise.

In the first place, problems are created for reviewing courts by discounting formal enactment as evidence of congressional decision among policy alternatives. It could be argued that the procedural formalities of Article I constitute, by law, the authoritative indices that decision has been reached. Unlike political scientists, judges and other citizens are entitled to count enactment as decision. A corollary problem concerns the power of Congress to defer decision in this manner. It could be argued with the Maryland Court in *Rice* v. *Foster* that "legislatures are vested with no power to pass an act which is not a law in itself when passed."[53] A further problem is the likelihood that some experimental delegations would present Congress not with material for policy choices of its own but with faits accomplis. Thus, Senator Thomas F. Eagleton read a section of the War Powers Act of 1973 as "an open-ended, blank check for 90 days of warmaking, anywhere in the world, by the President of the United States."[54] The provision requires congressional approval of troop commitments extending beyond a ninety-day period, permitting termination at an earlier point through concurrent resolution. Recalling congressional reluctance to end support of the Vietnam War while troops were engaged, Senator Eagleton evaluated the requirement of congressional approval as "shallow indeed," predicting congressional helplessness "[o]nce that flag was committed."[55]

Inevitably, it has also been remarked that in the nuclear age, "all too much decisiveness can occur within 90 minutes, much less 90 days."[56] And even if such difficulties were met, experimental delegations could still be challenged on other grounds. Decisions which are admittedly experimental or under authorizations of limited duration may not always possess sufficient authority to legitimize deprivations of life, liberty, and property. We need not dwell upon problems of sending troops to war, for example, under such delegations.

Moreover, difficult practical questions remain concerning the effectiveness of mandatory review and reenactment for the end sought. Are the political problems which constitute the subjects of broad delegations always amenable to treatment under relatively specific and stable statements of policy? How will the anticipation of review and reenactment affect agency performance relative to the development of such statements? And how realistic is the expectation that Congress will always be more prepared to accept the duty of decision after periods of administrative experimentation than before? There seems little basis for optimism in some of our more serious problems.

Consider, for example, congressional performance in the 1970–73 delegations to the president of authority to control wages and prices. The authority originated in an amendment to the Defense Production Act of 1970 amid partisan allegations of buck-passing over responsibility for controlling inflation. Congressional Democrats asserted that responsibility lay with the executive branch, while the president and members of his party were telling Congress that if it wanted controls it should mandate them.[57] In October of 1971 the president announced "Phase II," a program of mandatory controls following a wage-price freeze imposed the preceding August, and requested an immediate extension of authority to April 1973. Request for immediate extension came despite the lack of experience with Phase II and despite the opportunity to observe its operation in the remaining six months of statutory duration. The Democratic chairmen of the Joint Economic Committee and the House Currency and Banking Committee failed in their calls for Congress to review performance before extending authority.[58] The president got the extension. However, in actions revealing the continuing efforts of all to evade accountability, the president did not get his request for statutory ratification of his decisions up to that point. Phase III, a suspension of most mandatory controls, was announced in January 1973. At the same time the president asked for another extension of authority to April 1974. The president got this extension too, and without significant statutory conditions, despite loud complaints in Congress over the failure of the voluntary controls. Congressional threats of mandatory controls, freezes, and price rollbacks gave way to congressional irresolution. One congressman told the press, "I don't know any subject where we have less confidence in ourselves than in economics."[59] Things not dissimilar were being said about the executive branch.[60] By the year's end there was to be another round of freezes, controls, and disappointments. Without a further request for extension, control authority was permitted to expire in April 1974.

To the legal arguments against validating those overly broad delegations which are accompanied with provisions for mandatory review and reenactment, we answer, first, that the practice, if effective, could be compatible with the minimal criteria of the delegation doctrine. This is not to say that all of the values associated with the rule are satisfied by such provisions. Without debating the issue further we can say, secondly, that of the techniques for insulating delegations made from indecision relative to the most salient alternatives, mandatory review and reenactment is certainly less objectionable than the other methods we have discussed.

As for the uncertainty of provisions for mandatory review as effective means to eventual congressional decision, we come to the limits of this study. We note only that where and to what degrees the agencies and others would be able to help Congress make relatively clear and stable policy are matters of some disagreement among leading authorities on our subject.[61] Whether Congress will be able to overcome the electoral advantages of ducking responsibility for decision by committing itself to difficult burdens of choice, and whether it would be willing to use what aid others could provide, depend in part on the strength in Congress of the belief that there is a constitutional obligation to do so.

The most that we might hope to have established here is that as a matter of constitutional law such an obligation does exist. The duty not to abdicate the burden of decision seems an essential part of our idea of constitutional government. But the legal principle of nondelegation alone has proved unable to secure the adherence of Congress to its constitutional obligations. And this brings us back to an aspect of the delegation problem mentioned at the beginning of this study: whether and under what conditions we might realistically rely for the maintenance of our institution on a sense of duty among our officeholders—and among their constituents. This question directs us beyond the scope of the present discussion to a more interesting and fundamental part of the delegation problem.

Notes

Chapter 1

1. J. William Fulbright, "The Legislator: Congress and the War" (address delivered at the University of South Florida, Tampa, February 4, 1971).

2. Mark J. Green, James M. Fallows, and David R. Zwick, *Who Runs Congress?* (New York: Bantam Books, 1972), pp. 113-18.

3. *Time*, January 15, 1973, p. 11.

4. Panama Refining Co. v. Ryan, 293 U.S. 388 (1935); A. L. A. Schechter Poultry Corp. v. United States, 295 U.S. 495 (1935); Carter v. Carter Coal Co., 298 U.S. 238 (1936).

5. Henry J. Friendly, *The Federal Administrative Agencies: The Need for Better Definition of Standards* (Cambridge: Harvard University Press, 1962), pp. 22f., and see also pp. 6, 13, 163-73.

6. Louis L. Jaffe, *Judicial Control of Administrative Action* (Boston: Little, Brown, 1965), pp. 48-51.

7. Theodore J. Lowi, "The Public Philosophy: Interest-Group Liberalism," *APSR* 61 (March 1967): 18ff.; idem, *The End of Liberalism* (New York: W. W. Norton and Co., 1969), chap. 5.

8. James M. Landis, *The Administrative Process* (New Haven: Yale University Press, 1938), pp. 6, 59f.

9. Friendly, *The Federal Administrative Agencies,* pp. 167f.

10. *Time,* January 15, 1973, p. 12, quoting Senator Robert Packwood.

11. Jacob E. Cook, ed., *The Federalist* (Middletown, Conn.. Wesleyan University Press, 1961), p. 349. We could begin to analyze the delegation question from the extralegal perspective of the Framers by considering the problem of combining the personal interests of members of Congress with the rights of Congress as an institution. Whether reflecting the personal views of his creators or not, Publius would not have been surprised if a body like Congress were to evade its legal responsibilities in certain difficult political circumstances.

12. Green, Fallows, and Zwick, *Who Runs Congress?,* pp. 1-5.

Chapter 2

1. Article I, section 8 of the Constitution enumerates most of the specific powers Congress is authorized to exercise. Examples are the power "to lay and collect Taxes," to "regulate Commerce with foreign Nations, and among the several States," and to "declare War, grant Letters of Marque and Reprisal, and Make Rules concerning Captures on Land and Water." The last paragraph of this list is the "necessary and proper clause." It states that Congress shall have power "to make all Laws which shall be necessary and proper for carrying into Execution the foregoing Powers, and all other Powers vested by this Constitution in the Government of the United States, or in any Department or Officer thereof."

2. Kenneth Culp Davis, *Administrative Law Treatise* (St. Paul: West Publishing Co., 1958), secs. 2.01-.06, 2.14, 2.16. In a more recent work Davis urges revitalizing the delegation doctrine on a common-law basis for application to administrators rather than to legislatures. In his *Discretionary Justice* (Baton Rouge: Louisiana State University Press, 1969), chaps. 2 and 3, he argues that as historically applied to Congress the delegation doctrine was an unrealistic and unwise attempt to inhibit the development of discretionary authority on the basis of an "extravagant version of the rule of law" which doomed the delegation doctrine to failure. Nevertheless, Davis seems to feel that the original aim of limiting discretion was praiseworthy, if extravagant, and that a modified version of the delegation doctrine which aims at an ever-shifting

optimum mixture of discretion and rule should be adopted by the courts. The new delegation doctrine is not to be applied to legislative decisions, however. It is to serve as a means of requiring administrators to structure and confine their own discretion.

3. Patrick W. Duff and Horace E. Whiteside, "Delegata Potestas Non Potest Delegari: A Maxim of American Constitutional Law," *Cornell Law Quarterly* 14 (1929): 195.

4. Rocco J. Tresolini, *American Constitutional Law* (New York: Macmillan, 1965), pp. 154–58.

5. Carl J. Friedrich, *Constitutional Government and Democracy* (Waltham, Mass.: Blaisdell, 1960), p. 580.

6. John P. Roche, "Distribution of Powers," *International Encyclopedia of the Social Sciences*, 3 (1968), pp. 305–7.

7. Jackson's view that the rule of nondelegation is "purely judgemade, not Constitution made," is quoted in Carl B. Swisher, *American Constitutional Development* (Boston: Houghton Mifflin, 1954), p. 910.

8. Herman Pritchett, *The American Constitution* (New York: McGraw-Hill, 1968), p. 198; see also Davis, *Treatise,* secs. 2.02–.06.

9. Edward S. Corwin, *The Constitution and What It Means Today* (Princeton: Princeton University Press, 1946), p. 141. This comment on the substantive limitations of Article V appears to conflict (at least in spirit) with an earlier remark on the Preamble. Corwin notes on p. 2 that the Preamble speaks in the present tense and should therefore read that We the people " 'Do ordain and establish,' not *did* ordain and establish." From this he concludes that "As a *document* the Constitution came from the present generation of American citizens, and hence should be interpreted in the light of present conditions and with a view to meeting present problems." As a call for flexible interpretation within the limits of constitutional language, there is no point in quarreling with this statement. But if he intends to deny either that there are limits to interpretation or that constitutional limits bind generations subsequent to the founding generation—even in the face of their demands—then the least one can say is that there is contradiction between Corwin's theory of the Preamble and his theory of Article V.

10. K. C. Wheare, *Modern Constitutions* (London: Oxford University Press, 1966), pp. 77ff., 32f., 49ff., 54ff., 60, 97, 105, 137.

11. Cook, *The Federalist,* p. 147; cf. pp. 579f.

12. The attempt would deny the normal situation of disagreement

among individuals over which areas of decision to collectivize and how. See James M. Buchanan and Gordon Tullock, *The Calculus of Consent* (Ann Arbor: University of Michigan Press, 1962), pp. 82ff.

13. See Davis, *Treatise*, secs. 2.01-.06; Jaffe, *Judicial Control of Administrative Action*, pp. 51–73; and Pritchett, *The American Constitution*, pp. 198–203.

14. Edward S. Corwin, *The President: Office and Powers* (New York: New York University Press, 1948), pp. 110–13; Davis, *Treatise*, secs. 2.01, 2.16; cf. Landis "Delegata Potestas Non Potest Delegari," pp. 191f.

15. Duff and Whiteside, "Delegata Potestas Non Potest Delegari," pp. 191f.

16. 1 Cranch. 137, 176–79.

17. Roy P. Basler, ed., *Abraham Lincoln: His Speeches and Writings* (New York: Grosset & Dunlap, 1962), pp. 600f.; James G. Randall, *Constitutional Problems Under Lincoln* (Urbana: University of Illinois Press, 1964), pp. 34–41.

18. Oliver W. Holmes, "Law and the Court," *Collected Legal Papers* (New York: Harcourt, Brace, 1920), p. 295.

19. Davis, *Treatise*, sec. 2.01.

20. Cook, *The Federalist*, no. 33, pp. 204f.

21. Cf. Roche, "Distribution of Powers," pp. 305–7.

22. Davis, *Treatise*, sec. 2.16.

23. Roche, "Distribution of Powers," p. 307.

24. Wayman v. Southard, 10 Wheat. 1 (1825).

25. Pritchett, *The American Constitution*, p. 199.

26. See above, p. 65.

27. John P. Roche, "Executive Power and Domestic Emergency: The Quest for Prerogative," in Roche, *Shadow and Substance: Essays on the Theory and Structure of Politics* (New York: Macmillan, 1964), p. 127.

28. Ibid., p. 130.

29. 323 U.S. 214 (1944).

30. Roche, "Executive Power and Domestic Emergency," pp. 132f.

31. Ibid.

32. Pritchett, *The American Constitution*, p. 199.

33. See above, n. 14, chap. 2.

34. Robert E. Cushman, *The Independent Regulatory Commissions* (New York: Oxford University Press, 1941), p. 427.

35. An example of this tendency is shown by Davis when he says that the rule represents a simplistic attempt to divide power neatly once and for all between legislative and administrative authorities; see above, n. 2, chap. 2. See also James Hart, *An Introduction to Administrative Law* (New York: Appleton-Century-Crofts, 1950), p. 314, and J. Roland Pennock, *Administration and the Rule of Law* (New York: Rinehart & Co., 1941), pp. 119 f.

36. James Kent, *Commentaries on American Law,* ed. by John M. Gould, 14th ed. (Boston: Little Brown, 1896), 2: 633f.

37. G. Burdeau, "Delegation of Powers," *International Encyclopedia of the Social Sciences,* 4 (1968), p. 74.

38. Locke, *Second Treatise,* sec. 141; *The Federalist,* nos. 1, 49, 78; U.S. Constitution, Preamble, Ninth and Tenth Amendments; see also Pritchett's comments on United States v. Curtiss-Wright Export Corporation, 299 U.S. 304 (1936), in *The American Constitution,* p. 355.

39. Cf. Peter Woll, *American Bureaucracy* (New York: Norton, 1963), pp. 110ff.

40. Duff and Whiteside, "Delegata Potestas Non Potest Delegari," p. 168.

41. Ibid., pp. 168–73.

42. Ibid., pp. 173ff., 194ff., 195 n. 91.

43. Ibid., pp. 195f.

44. I am following Jaffe's reconstruction of our author's point in *Judicial Control of Administrative Action,* p. 54 n. 60; cf. Duff and Whiteside, "Delegata Potestas Non Potest Delegari," pp. 172f.

45. Duff and Whiteside, "Delegata Potestas Non Potest Delegari," p. 191 n. 78a.

46. Ibid., p. 192: in one place they say that the maxim applies to "abdication"; in another they say that abdication is "more than delegation."

47. Ibid.

48. Horst P. Ehmke, " 'Delegata Potestas Non Potest Delegari' A Maxim of American Constitutional Law," *Cornell Law Quarterly* 47 (1961): 50.

49. Jaffe, *Judicial Control of Administrative Action,* p. 54, quoting Locke, *Second Treatise,* sec. 142.

50. Ibid.

51. Rodney L. Mott, *Due Process of Law* (Indianapolis: Bobbs-Merrill, 1926), p. 86.

52. Ibid., p. 86 n. 57.

53. The Federal Constitution does not prohibit the legislatures of the states from delegating their powers; it does prohibit state agencies from denying certain individual rights subsumed by the idea of due process.

54. John D. McGowen, "An Economic Interpretation of the Doctrine of Delegation of Governmental Powers," *Tulane Law Review* 12 (1968): 196-97; cf. Maurice H. Merrill, "Standards—A Safeguard for the Exercise of Delegated Power," *Nebraska Law Review* 47 (1968): 469-71.

55. Robert E. Cushman, "The Constitutional Status of the Independent Regulatory Commissions," *Cornell Law Quarterly* 24 (1938): 32-33.

56. Davis, *Discretionary Justice*, p. 217.

57. Ibid., pp. 219, 54-59.

58. Ibid., pp. 45-50.

59. Kunz v. New York, 340 U.S. 290 (1951), invalidating the ordinance as a prior restraint on the exercise of First Amendment rights.

60. Gooding v. Wilson, 405 U.S. 518 (1972), finding vagueness and overbreadth in language not confined by state courts to "fighting words" tending to incite "an immediate breach of the peace."

61. Kent v. Dulles, 357 U.S. 116 (1958), narrowly construing the scope of the delegation to avoid considering substantive Fifth Amendment questions raised by State Department restrictions on Communist applicants.

62. Cf. Alexander M. Bickel, *The Least Dangerous Branch* (Indianapolis: Bobbs-Merrill, 1962), pp. 159-61, 164-69.

63. Jaffe, *Judicial Control of Administrative Action*, p. 93.

64. Thomas M. Cooley, *Constitutional Limitations* (Boston: Little, Brown, 1903), p. 163.

65. Sec. 142.

66. Woll, *American Bureaucracy*, p. 138.

67. Ibid., pp. 139f.

68. Cf. Duff and Whiteside, "Delegata Potestas Non Potest Delegari," pp. 177ff., and the extensive quote from Rice v. Foster, 4 Harr. 479 (Del. 1847).

69. Cf. Malcolm Sharp, "The Classical American Doctrine of 'The

Separation of Powers,' " *Selected Essays on Constitutional Law,* Association of American Law Schools (Chicago: Foundation Press, 1938), p. 168.

70. Cf. Davis, *Treatise* (1970 supp.) secs. 2.00–2.03, and *Discretionary Justice,* pp. 41, 46, 49ff. Davis's new effort to revitalize the rule of nondelegation seems based on a denial of the proposition that Congress has duties it should not be permitted to evade. A belief that no "authority other than the electorate" should "try to require Congress to legislate in greater detail than it is inclined to" is one of the factors in his conclusion that the rule should shift from a requirement of legislative standards to one of administrative standards. But this approach, while possibly useful for those who emphasize the structuring of discretionary authority, has two conceptual weaknesses: first, it reduces nondelegation to an aspect of due process, and, second, it so construes the rule as to render it inapplicable to Congress. The new delegation doctrine would have no direct application either to the legislature or to acts of delegation. A radically new understanding of the rule thus seems the price for its restoration as a tool for "minimizing injustice from improper discretionary power." For comments on the realism of Davis's expectation that the courts will be more successful in requiring standards from administrators than they have been from legislators, see Jaffe's review of *Discretionary Justice* in the *Villanova Law Review* 14 (1969): 773.

71. Cook, *The Federalist,* no. 48, p. 332.

72. Ibid., pp. 333f.

73. Cf. Woll, *American Bureaucracy,* pp. 18ff.

74. Cook, *The Federalist,* no. 51, pp. 347–51.

75. Ibid., no. 10, pp. 59ff.; no. 49, pp. 344ff.; no. 50, pp. 358ff.; no 72, pp. 488ff.

76. Ibid., no. 51, p. 349.

77. Ibid.

78. Cf. John B. Cheadle, "The Delegation of Legislative Functions," *Yale Law Journal* 27 (1918): 896–97.

79. Ibid., pp. 900f.

80. 1 Cranch. 137, at 177 (1803).

81. 4 Wheat. 316, at 421 (1819).

82. Basler, *Abraham Lincoln: His Speeches and Writings,* p. 608.

83. Wilfred E. Binkley, *President and Congress* (New York: Vintage Books, 1962), pp. 293.

84. Jaffe's criticism of Ernst Freund is instructive at this point. In 1928 Freund said, "While it is extremely difficult to formulate a generally valid principle of legitimacy of delegation, the observation may be hazarded, that with regard to major matters the appropriate sphere of delegated authority is where there are no controverted issues of policy or of opinion." Of this Jaffe remarks that it is "demonstrably too narrow to describe legislative phenomena or to fulfill political need." Later he suggests that Freund's formulation is "in a sense a counsel of laissez faire" since Congress could not delegate at all in many fields if it were compelled to settle all policy conflicts. However this is not to be taken as a suggestion on Jaffe's part that Congress is free to delegate without settling the overarching issues of policy. In his summary of the "occasions for delegating power to administrative officers," he says: "They can be compassed by a single generalization. Power should be delegated where there is agreement that a task must be performed and it cannot be effectively performed by the legislature without the assistance of a delegate." This and subsequent statements suggest that delegations should be instrumental to substantive decisions at some level, even if only after periods of administrative experimentation. Jaffe, *Judicial Control of Administrative Action*, pp. 34, 35 n. 15, 37, 39, 41f.

85. Cf. Landis, *The Administrative Process*, p. 52.

86. See Louis Fisher, "Presidential Spending Discretion and Congressional Controls" (Delivered at APSA Annual Meeting, Chicago, 1971), pp. 14f.

87. Cf. Green, Fallows, and Zwick, *Who Runs Congress?*, pp. 115.

88. 31 U.S.C. sec. 665 (c)(2).

89. Cf. Green, Fallows, and Zwick, *Who Runs Congress?*, pp. 114ff.

90. 92nd Cong., 1st Sess., Report of Hearings, March 24, 1971, pp. 174-81.

91. Ibid., p. 176.

92. Ibid., pp. 174-76.

93. Ibid., p. 176.

94. Ibid., p. 177.

95. Ibid.

96. Ibid., p. 176.

97. Ibid., p. 177.

98. Dean Alfange, Jr., "Free Speech and Symbolic Conduct: The Draft-Card Burning Case," *1968 Supreme Court Review,* pp. 27–38.

99. 6 Cranch. 87 (1810).

100. Alfange, "Free Speech and Symbolic Conduct," pp. 27–31.

101. Ibid., pp. 31–35.

102. Ibid., p. 37.

103. Ibid., pp. 35f., and cf. Carl A. Auerback and Lloyd K. Garrison, *The Legal Process* (San Francisco: Chandler, 1961), pp. 842ff.

104. Alfange, "Free Speech and Symbolic Conduct," pp. 27ff.

105. Ibid., pp. 36ff.

106. Ibid., p. 31.

107. Ibid., and cf. Auerback and Garrison, *The Legal Process,* p. 838, n. 7.

108. Carter v. Carter Coal Co., 298 U.S. 238 (1936).

109. See United States v. Sharpnack 355 U.S. 286 (1958), Douglas and Black dissenting.

110. See above, pp. 60f.

111. Bickel, *The Least Dangerous Branch,* p. 151.

112. Davis, *Treatise,* sec. 2.05.

Chapter 3

1. 7 Cranch. 383.

2. 143 U.S. 649.

3. 7 Cranch. 383, at 383, 384.

4. Ibid., at 386.

5. Ibid., at 387.

6. Ibid., at 388.

7. See below, n. 19, chap. 3.

8. By the time *Aurora* was decided, the world was aware that Madison's proclamation, whatever the original congressional assumptions and intent, had been based on a policy choice of a rather important and controversial variety, as we shall see.

9. Pritchett, *The American Constitution,* p. 200.

10. 143 U.S. 649, at 693, 694.

11. Jaffe, *Judicial Control of Administrative Action,* p. 56.

12. Ibid., p. 52. President Madison claimed in a message to Congress, December 5, 1810, that the proclamation was issued not according to presidential discretion but "as prescribed by law." However, in a letter to Jefferson of March 18, 1811, he admitted an

understanding of the situation which belies this claim. See Henry Adams, *History of the United States of America* (New York: Antiquarian Press, 1962), 5:317f., 349f.; Edward Channing, *A History of the United States* (New York: Macmillan, 1917), 4:412.

13. Channing, *A History of the United States,* p. 413.

14. Ibid.

15. Ibid., p. 415.

16. Samuel Eliot Morison, *The Oxford History of the American People* (New York: Oxford University Press, 1965), p. 378; cf. Adams, *History of the United States of America,* 5: 350.

17. Adams, *History of the United States of America,* 5: 304.

18. Ibid., pp. 339f.

19. Ibid., pp. 351-54. This act has been mentioned above as a possible factor in the Court's approach to the delegation problem in *The Brig Aurora.*

20. Ibid., pp. 349f.

21. 20 Annals 1195 (1810).

22. 143 U.S. 649, at 680.

23. Ibid., at 692, 693.

24. *Judicial Control of Administrative Action,* p. 56.

25. 143 U.S. 649, at 692.

26. 4 Harr. 479 (Del. 1847), cited by Duff and Whiteside, "Delegata Potestas Non Potest Delegari," p. 177.

27. Duff and Whiteside, "Delegata Potestas Non Potest Delegari," p. 178.

28. Ibid., pp. 178ff.

29. 6 Barr. 507 (Pa. 1847); Duff and Whiteside, "Delegata Potestas Non Potest Delegari," p. 181.

30. 72 Pa. 491 (1873); Duff and Whiteside, "Delegata Potestas Non Potest Delegari," pp. 182f.

31. Duff and Whiteside, "Delegata Potestas Non Potest Delegari," pp. 181-90.

32. Ibid., p. 184; Davis, *Treatise,* 2.07.

33. 143 U.S. 649, at 692.

34. Frank W. Taussig, *The Tariff History of the United States* (New York: G. P. Putnam's Sons, 1892), p. 283.

35. Ibid., p. 278.

36. Ibid., pp. 186, 275, 279.

37. 21 Cong. Rec. 10587, 10588, 10591 (1890).

38. 10 Wheat. 1 (1825).

39. 3 Annals 1388, 1389 (1792).

40. Swisher, *American Constitutional Development*, p. 216.

41. Charles Warren, *The Supreme Court in United States History* (Boston: Little, Brown, 1947), 1: 647ff.

42. Ibid., p. 650.

43. Ibid., pp. 650f.

44. 10 Wheat. 1, at 43–46.

45. Cf. Pritchett, *The American Constitution*, p. 199.

46. 4 Cong. Rec. 348 (1828).

47. Ibid., at 356.

48. 10 Wheat. 1, at 46–47.

49. 4 Cong. Rec. 350 (1828).

50. 3 Annals 85 (1792).

51. Ibid., at 581, 582.

52. Ibid., at 582.

53. Ibid., at 594.

54. Ibid., at 599.

55. Ibid., at 138, 159.

56. People v. Reynolds, 10 Ill. 1 (1848).

57. 192 U.S. 470.

58. 276 U.S. 394.

59. Ibid., at 409.

60. Jaffe, *Judicial Control of Administrative Action*, pp. 59f.

61. 48 L. Ed. 531.

62. Ibid., at 533.

63. Ibid.

64. 192 U.S. 470, at 496.

65. 29 Cong. Rec. 2244 (1897).

66. Ibid., at 2390.

67. Pritchett, *The American Constitution*, p. 200.

68. 276 U.S. 394, at 401, 402.

69. Ibid., at 404.

70. Ibid., at 406.

71. Ibid., at 410, 411.

72. Ibid., at 406.

73. Ibid., at 409.

74. John Day Larkin, *The President's Control of the Tariff* (Cambridge: Harvard University Press, 1936), pp. 132ff., 134f.

75. Taussig, *The Tariff History of the United States*, pp. 447–53.

76. Larkin, *The President's Control of the Tariff*, p. 109.

77. 62 Cong. Rec. 1152–54 (1922).

78. Ibid., at 11157, 11160, 11183; Larkin, *The President's Control of the Tariff,* pp. 132–34.

79. *The President's Control of the Tariff,* pp. 138f.

80. Ibid., pp. 139f.

81. Ibid., p. 144.

82. Ibid., pp. 132ff., 144f. Larkin reports that the Tariff Commission was to be divided on the question of including transportation costs. On request of the president, the attorney general ended the wrangling within the commission with an opinion that transportation costs should be taken into account in determining production costs.

83. Ibid., pp. 113, 184, 191–94.

84. Ibid., p. 194.

85. Ibid., p. 110, n. 20.

86. 293 U.S. 389.

87. 295 U.S. 495.

88. Jaffe, *Judicial Control of Administrative Action,* p. 60; Pritchett, *The American Constitution,* p. 200.

89. Jackson, *Struggle for Judicial Supremacy,* p. 92.

90. 293 U.S. 389, at 406.

91. Ibid., at 415, 416.

92. Ibid., at 421.

93. Ibid.

94. Ibid., at 422–430.

95. Ibid., at 418.

96. Ibid., at 434.

97. Ibid., at 434, 435.

98. 48 Stat. at L. 195.

99. 293 U.S. 389, at 418.

100. Ibid., at 431.

101. Ibid., at 438. As we shall see, Cardozo, in order to provide for the conflict between the several aims of the statute posited in Section 1 (a chief point of the majority opinion), eventually was forced to construct a standard even less specific than those in the statute. This attempt to defend a more general standard as an effective guideline for executive discretion brought him to unworkable distinctions and contradiction.

102. Ibid., at 418.

103. Ibid., at 438.

104. 48 Stat. at L. 196.

105. Cf. Leverett S. Lyon, ed., *The National Recovery Administration* (Washington: The Brookings Institution, 1935), pp. 293ff.

106. 293 U.S. 389, at 436.

107. 77 Cong. Rec. 5015, 5292-5299 (1933).

108. 79 Cong. Rec. 2128, 2131, 2136, 2458 (1935).

109. Ibid., at 2458, 2501-2.

110. 295 U.S. 495, at 529, 530, 541, 542.

111. Ibid., at 553.

112. Jaffe, *Judicial Control of Administrative Action,* pp. 67-70.

113. 48 Stat. at L. 196.

114. 295 U.S. 495, at 531, 532, 541.

115. Ibid., at 552.

116. Ibid., at 552, 553.

117. 293 U.S. 389, at 418.

118. Ibid., at 421, 430.

119. Ibid., at 436.

120. Ibid., at 438.

121. Cf. Woll, *American Bureaucracy,* pp. 116-120.

122. Ellis W. Hawley, *The New Deal and the Problem of Monopoly* (Princeton: Princeton University Press, 1966), pp. 21-26.

123. Ibid., pp. 26ff.

124. Ibid., pp. 20, 33.

125. Ibid., p. 33.

126. Arthur M. Schlesinger, Jr., *The Coming of the New Deal* (Boston: Houghton Mifflin, 1958), pp. 100ff.

127. 77 Cong. Rec. 4202 (1933).

128. Ibid., at 4206.

129. Ibid., at 4206, 4336.

130. Ibid., at 4206.

131. Ibid., at 4207.

132. Ibid., at 4326; see also Watson's remarks at 4211, and Beck's remarks at 4213, 4216.

133. Ibid., remarks by Vinson, at 4223; by Knutson, at 4227; by Jenkins, at 4322; by Treadway, at 4328; by Shullenberger, at 4331; and by Evans, at 4347.

134. Ibid., at 4222.

135. Ibid., at 4373.

136. Ibid., remarks by Borah, at 5162-66; and by Black, at 5238-39.

137. Ibid., at 5152, 5153.

138. Schlesinger, *The Coming of the New Deal,* p. 100.

139. 77 Cong. Rec. 5425.

140. Ibid., at 5425.

141. Hugh S. Johnson, *The Blue Eagle from Egg to Earth* (Garden City, N.Y.: Doubleday, 1935), p. 184.

142. Ibid., pp. 181f.

143. 77 Cong. Rec. 5835, 5836 (1933).

144. Ibid., at 5838, 5694.

145. Ibid., at 5694.

146. Ibid., at 5845.

147. Schlesinger, *The Coming of the New Deal,* chap. 8.

148. Ibid., pp. 122f.

149. Ibid., p. 125.

150. Ibid., pp. 126ff.; and Hawley, *The New Deal and the Problem of Monopoly,* p. 73.

151. Schlesinger, *The Coming of the New Deal,* pp. 130f.; and Hawley, *The New Deal and the Problem of Monopoly,* pp. 72–81, 85, 87f.

152. Schlesinger, *The Coming of the New Deal,* pp. 132–35; and Hawley, *The New Deal and the Problem of Monopoly,* pp. 90, 93–97.

153. Hawley, *The New Deal and the Problem of Monopoly,* p. 95.

154. Ibid., pp. 98ff.; Schlesinger, *The Coming of the New Deal,* p. 135.

155. Hawley, *The New Deal and The Problem of Monopoly,* pp. 101ff., 106–10.

156. Ibid., pp. 33f., quoting Ernest K. Lindley, *Halfway with Roosevelt* (New York: Viking, 1937), p. 156.

157. 298 U.S., 238.

158. Ibid., at 311.

159. Ibid.

160. See above, pp. 39f.

161. 307 U.S. 533.

162. Ibid., at 574–77; 307 U.S. 588, at 606.

163. 307 U.S. 588, at 606.

164. 321 U.S. 414.

165. Ibid., at 420.

166. Ibid., at 451, 452.

167. Lichter v. United States, 334 U.S. 742, at 774–87.

168. Woll, American Bureaucracy, pp. 116f.

169. Jaffe, *Judicial Control of Administrative Action,* p. 71.

170. Davis, *Discretionary Justice*, pp. 41, 49ff., 466; and *Treatise* (1970 supp.), sec. 2.00.

171. See above, p. 89.

172. Jaffe, *Judicial Control of Administrative Action*, p. 71; cf. Davis on *Lichter*, in *Treatise*, sec. 2.03.

173. Jaffe, *Judicial Control of Administrative Action*, p. 71.

174. See above, pp. 32f.

175. Burstyn v. Wilson, 343 U.S. 495 (1952).

176. Saia v. New York, 334 U.S. 558 (1948).

177. Watkins v. United States, 354 U.S. 178 (1957).

178. 357 U.S. 116.

179. Ibid., at 128, 129.

180. Ibid., at 129.

181. Ibid., at 138-143.

182. Ibid., at 130.

183. *American Foreign Policy: Current Documents*, 1964, p. 980.

184. Ibid.

185. Ibid., p. 981. See also the president's message to Congress, 110 Cong. Rec. 18132 (1964). The accuracy of the administration's description and interpretation of the events in the Gulf of Tonkin in early August has been the subject of extensive controversy. See Peter Dale Scott, "Tonkin Bay: Was There a Conspiracy?" review of James C. Goulden, *Truth is the First Casualty: The Gulf of Tonkin Affair—Illusion and Reality*, in the *New York Review of Books*, January 29, 1970, pp. 31-40. See also 110 Cong. Rec. 18134, 18423-25 (1964), for congressional expressions of doubt at the time.

186. 51 Dept. of State Bulletin 268 (1964).

187. 110 Cong. Rec. 18471, 18555 (1964).

188. Eugene Eidenberg, "The President: Americanizing the War in Vietnam," in Allan P. Sindler, ed., *American Political Institutions and Public Policy* (Boston: Little, Brown, 1969), pp. 98-103.

189. 110 Cong. Rec. 18133-18139, 18413, 18423, 18430, 18442-18456 (1964).

190. 110 Cong. Rec. 18399 (1964) (Sen. Mansfield), 18400, 18402, 18404, 18457, 18458 (Sen. Fulbright), 18411 (Sen. Russell), 18415 (Sen. Stennis), 18416 (Sen. Church), 18418 (Sen. Cooper), 18421 (Sen. Humphrey), 18462 (Sen. Dirksen), 18539 (Rep. Morgan), 18542 (Rep. Albert), 18542 (Rep. Halleck).

191. 111 Cong. Rec. 9106-13, 9117-19 (1965) (Sen. Morse),

9729–9752 (Sen. Gruening).

192. Hearings Before the Senate Subcommittee on Separation of Powers, 90th Cong., 1st Sess. (July 19, 1967).

193. Ibid., at 47.

194. Ibid.

195. 389 U.S. 934 (1967).

196. Ibid., at 935.

197. Roger H. Hull and John C. Novogrod, *Law and Vietnam* (Dobbs Ferry: Oceans Publications, Inc., 1968), pp. 168–78; *National Commitments: Report on S. Res. 187,* 90th Cong., 1st Sess. at 21–22 (November 20, 1967).

198. 62 Dept. of State Bulletin 468 (1970).

199. Ibid., at 761.

200. 110 Cong. Rec. 18136, 18138 (1964) (Sen. Morse), 18403, 18406–18410 (Sen. Fulbright), 18548 (Rep. Barry), 18551 (Rep. Reuss).

201. Ibid., at 18402 (Senators McGovern, Brewster, and Fulbright), 18403 (Sen. Nelson), 18134, 18137, 18427 (Sen. Morse), 18457 (Sen. Javits).

202. Almost every comment made during the debate contained, explicitly or implicitly, some form of the limited-war alternative. Since the president had interpreted his actions and the intended scope of his future actions as within the limited-war concept, every statement and every vote in support of the resolution can be construed as having accepted a limited involvement at least. As the war progressed through the retaliatory air strikes of late 1964, to the continuous air strikes announced in early 1965, and to the troop decisions of July of that year and beyond, the operational meaning of "limited war" became a matter of heated debate. Because we are looking at the salient alternatives before Congress *prior* to the Americanization of the war, we are treating "limited war" as a relatively limited range of possibilities which was more or less distinguishable from other possibilities. In the minds of many it did not prove to be so with the military escalations of the months to come, but during the debate in August 1964, the concept of limited war was distinguishable from other concepts.

203. 110 Cong. Rec. 18084, 18181, 18194, 18201, 18335, 18417 (1964).

204. Ibid., at 18243, 18447, 18461.

205. Ibid., at 18135, 18138.

206. Ibid., at 18458 (colloquy between Senators Fulbright and Nelson), 18551 (Rep. Reuss).

207. Ibid., at 18133–39.

208. Ibid., at 18421.

209. Eidenberg, *The President: Americanizing the War in Vietnam*, pp. 96f., notes that the Gallup poll of October 4, 1964, reported that three in ten Republicans had defected to the Democratic presidential candidate due to a fear of Senator Goldwater's hawkish proposals for the Vietnam conflict. As early as March 4 Senator Goldwater had called for carrying the air war to North Vietnam and the use of low-yield nuclear weapons to remove the protective foliage of Communist supply routes. We might speculate that the effectiveness of President Johnson's efforts to depict his opponent as reckless and irresponsible was felt in Congress during the Tonkin debate by those who might otherwise have openly proposed war with the North.

210. 110 Cong. Rec. 18190 (1964) (Rep. Sikes), 18408 (Sen. Scott), 18546 (Rep. Ashbrook), 18547 (Reps. Derwinski and Foreman), 18548 (Rep. Laird), 18551 (Rep. Ford).

211. Ibid., at 18402 (Senators McGovern, Brewster, and Fulbright), 18403 (colloquy between Senators Fulbright and Nelson).

212. Ibid., at 18404.

213. Ibid.: see above, n. 190, chap. 3.

214. 110 Cong. Rec. 18403 (1964).

215. Ibid., at 18402–10, 18409.

216. Ibid., at 18459.

217. Ibid.

218. *National Commitments: Report on S. Res. 187,* 90th Cong., 1st Sess., at 20 (November 20, 1967).

219. 110 Cong. Rec. 18553 (1964).

220. *National Commitments: Report on S. Res. 187,* 90th Cong., 1st. Sess., at 21 (November 20, 1967).

221. See above, n. 188, chap. 3.

222. For examples both of the confusion on this point and of an unwillingness to clarify it, see 110 Cong. Rec. 18410, 18415, 18417, 18419, 18420, 18462, 18442, 18443, 18447, 18539, 18543, 18548 (1964).

223. J. William Fulbright, "The Legislator: Congress and the War" (address delivered at the University of South Florida, Tampa, February 4, 1971).

224. *National Commitments: Report on S. Res. 187,* 90th Cong., 1st Sess., at 19–20 (November 20, 1967).

Chapter 4

1. Davis, *Treatise* (1970 supp.), 2.04; cf. Joseph P. Harris, *Congressional Control of Administration* (Washington: Brookings Institution, 1964), pp. 8–11; cf. Jaffe, *Judicial Control of Administrative Action,* pp. 45f.

2. Compare the War Powers Act of November 1973, enabling Congress to terminate by concurrent resolution presidential commitment of troops abroad prior to the sixty- to ninety-day limit set by the act for commitments not authorized by Congress. *Congressional Quarterly Weekly Report,* November 10, 1973, p. 2943.

3. Harris, *Congressional Control of Administration,* p. 245.

4. Ibid., p. 204.

5. Ibid., pp. 238f.

6. Joseph Cooper and Ann Cooper, "The Legislative Veto and the Constitution," *George Washington Law Review* 30 (1964): 467.

7. Ibid., p. 474.

8. Jonathan Elliot, ed., *Debates on the Adoption of the Federal Constitution* (Washington: by the author, 1861), 5:431: "Mr. Madison, observing that if the negative of the President was confined to *bills,* it would be evaded by acts under the form and name of resolutions, votes, etc., proposed" an amendment which eventuated in the present language of Section 7(3); see Randolph's motion, in ibid., p. 431.

9. Section 7(3): "Every order, resolution, or vote to which the concurrence of the Senate and House of Representatives may be necessary (except on a question of Adjournment) shall be presented to the President of the United States; and before the same shall take effect, shall be approved by him, or being disapproved by him, shall be repassed by two-thirds of the Senate and House of Representatives, according to the Rules and Limitations prescribed in the case of a bill."

10. Harris, *Congressional Control of Administration,* pp. 239f.

11. Hollingsworth v Virginia, 3 Dall. 378, at 381 (1798).

12. Cooper and Cooper, "The Legislative Veto and the Constitution," p. 477.

13. Cooper and Cooper, "The Legislative Veto and the Constitution," pp. 474f.

14. Harris, *Congressional Control of Administration*, p. 241.

15. Cooper and Cooper, "The Legislative Veto and the Constitution," p. 478.

16. Compare testimony of Arthur Maass before the Senate Subcommittee on Separation of Powers, 90th Cong. 1st Sess. (July 19, 1967), pp. 189f.

17. Cooper and Cooper, "The Legislative Veto and the Constitution," pp. 514ff.

18. Ibid.

19. Harris, *Congressional Control of Administration*, p. 244.

20. Cooper and Cooper, "The Legislative Veto and the Constitution," pp. 508ff.; Michael W. Kirst, *Government Without Passing Laws* (Chapel Hill: University of North Carolina Press, 1969), pp. 85 ff.

21. Kirst, *Government Without Passing Laws,* pp. 84, 89; and Harris, *Congressional Control of Administration,* p. 86.

22. Arthur W. Macmahon, "Congressional Oversight of Administration: The Power of the Purse," in Theodore J. Lowi, ed., *Legislative Politics U.S.A.* (Boston: Little, Brown, 1962), p. 272.

23. Kirst, *Government Without Passing Laws,* p. 84.

24. Ibid., pp. 84–87.

25. Ibid., p. 85.

26. Ibid., pp. 23–30.

27. Macmahon, "Congressional Oversight of Administration: The Power of the Purse," p. 276.

28. Ibid., p. 277, and Kirst, *Government Without Passing Laws,* pp. 31, 39–44, 50–57.

29. Macmahon, "Congressional Oversight of Administration: The Power of the Purse," pp. 277f., and Kirst, *Government Without Passing Laws,* pp. 33f., 87.

30. Kirst, *Government Without Passing Laws,* pp. 87, 94, 97.

31. Ibid., pp. 47–50.

32. Macmahon, "Congressional Oversight of Administration: The Power of the Purse," pp. 278ff.

33. Kirst, *Government Without Passing Laws,* pp. 58ff.

34. Ibid., pp. 153–55.

35. Ibid., pp. 155f.

36. Ibid., pp. 159f.

37. Ibid., pp. 65-70, 79, and Harris, *Congressional Control of Administration*, pp. 81f., 88.

38. Harris, *Congressional Control of Administration*, p. 86.

39. Kirst, *Government Without Passing Laws*, p. 72.

40. Ibid., pp. 109-15.

41. Harris, *Congressional Control of Administration*, pp. 89f.

42. Kirst, *Government Without Passing Laws*, pp. 79f.

43. Cornelius P. Cotter, "Legislative Oversight," in Alfred de Grazia, *Congress: The First Branch of Government* (Washington: American Enterprise Institute for Public Policy Research, 1966), pp. 64-68.

44. Cf. ibid., pp. 32f.

45. Pritchett, *The American Constitution*, pp. 214ff.

46. Harris, *Congressional Control of Administration*, p. 9.

47. Cotter, "Legislative Oversight," p. 65f.

48. Ibid., p. 59.

49. Ibid., pp. 59f.

50. Ibid., pp. 59-64.

51. Ibid., p. 60.

52. Harris, *Congressional Control of Administration*, pp. 212f., 238-41.

53. 4 Harr. 479, at 492 (1847), quoted by Duff and Whiteside, "Delegata Potestas Non Potest Delegari," p. 180.

54. 119 Cong. Rec. S18992, Oct. 10, 1973.

55. Ibid., at S18993.

56. *Time*, November 19, 1973, p. 30.

57. *1970 Congressional Quarterly Almanac*, pp. 433-35.

58. Ibid., p. 459.

59. *Congressional Quarterly Weekly Report*, April 21, 1973, p. 939, quoting Rep. Richard T. Hanna.

60. *Newsweek*, April 23, 1973, pp. 81f.

61. To Davis's proposal for revitalizing the rule of nondelegation as a judicial doctrine that administrators define and structure their own discretion (see above, nn. 2, 70, chap. 2.), Jaffe responds that sometimes, in antitrust law, for example, discretion "is far more resistant to prior definition than he is prepared to presume." Jaffe indicates, however, that his disagreement with Davis's proposal does not concern its "underlying thesis," but "the degree to which the thesis is pressed" (Jaffe's review of *Discretionary Justice*, in *Villanova Law Review* 14 [1969]: 733-55, 788).

Index